Strength Manual For Running

Strength Manual For Running

By

Louie Simmons

STRENGTH MANUAL FOR RUNNING

Published by Westside4Athletes®
Made in United States Of America.
2017

Copyright © 2017 by Westside Barbell
Cover credit: Tom Barry
Back cover credit: Tom Barry

ISBN-13: 978-0-9973925-1-7

www.westside-barbell.com
Email: customercare@westside-barbell.com

Printed by Action Printing

LOUIE SIMMONS

DEDICATION

This book is dedicated to those who want to learn.

"It is better to be a warrior in a garden than to be a gardener in a war"

– Unknown

EPIGRAPH

Train Optimal

THE AUTHOR

Louie Simmons is the founder of the Columbus Ohio Westside Barbell Club, established 1986. Louie has several decades of special strength training experience for many sports. His members have broken over 100 all time worlds records in powerlifting. He has been a consultant for many collegiate and professional teams. He is one of only four men to have made elite totals in five weight classes, top 10 from 1971 to 2005, has authored eight books, 15 DVDs, 250 articles as well as being a current lecturer and holding 11 United States patents.

Table of Contents

THE AUTHOR ix

TABLE OF CONTENTS xi

ACKNOWLEDGEMENT xvii

PREFACE xix

CHAPTER 1: INTRODUCTION: LEARNING WHAT AN ATHLETE NEEDS 1
   Too Many Injuries 1
   Getting Better 2
   Recovery 3
   Use New Improved Training Methods 3

CHAPTER 2: FUNDAMENTALS TO CONTEMPLATE 5
   Delayed Transmutation 10

CHAPTER 3: PERIODIZATION—DIVISION INTO TRAINING PERIODS 11
   Three-Week Speed Strength Waves 11
   Volume And Intensity Zones 12
   Four Direct Periods Of Periodization 15
   The Importance Of Observation 15
   Eliminating Accommodation 16
   Nine-Week Training Cycle 16
   More Wave Cycle Discussion 21
   Monitoring Progress With The Westside System 22
   The Plan: From A 400- To A 1,000-Pound Squat 400-Pound Max Squat ... 23
   Band Jerk And Press Workout For Speed Strength 26
   Periodization By Percentages 27
   Four Examples Of A Three-Week Wave 300-Pound Max Clean/Snatch ... 30
   Speed Pulls 32
      1. Speed Pulls On Floor With Bands 32
      700-Pound Deadlift 32

2. Ultra-Wide Sumo Deadlifts With Bar Weight 700-Pound Deadlift 33
3. Box Deadlifts 33
350-Pound Deadlift 33
Example: 35
250-Pound Power Snatch 35
How To Change Volume At The Same Intensity Zone 39
500-Pound Max Front Squat 39
600-Pound Max Safety Squat Bar 39
700-Pound Max Regular Squat Bar 39
Circa Max Performed To A Parallel Box. 40
Delayed Transformation Connecting Circa-Max Phase 41
Workouts 42
Progress Is Based On Periodization 44
Special Exercises: 46

CHAPTER 4: FUNDAMENTALS OF JUMPING 49
Kneeling Jumps... 49
Combinations Of Resistance Jumping Methods..................................... 50
Jumping Methods 50
Box Squat Jumping.. 50
Methods Of Resistance 51
Depth Jumps 52
Depth Jump Correctly 53
How Do Depth Jumps Work? 54
Basic Physics. 54
Jumping Instructions 54
Special Jumps... 57

CHAPTER 5: WEIGHTED SLED PROGRAMING 59
Acceleration Workouts 59
Workouts For Maintaining Top Speed... 59
Power Walking Style.. 60
Added Resistance... 61

CHAPTER 6: ENDURANCE 63
Repetitive Training.. 65
Circuit Training 72
Continuous with Variable Intensity.. 72
Strength Endurance 73
Dynamic Endurance 74

General Endurance 74
General Endurance Training 75

CHAPTER 7: CONJUGATE SEQUENCE SYSTEM 79
Accomodating Resistance 81
Combinations Of Resistance Methods 81
    Band Tension 82
    Speed Strength 82
    Strength Speed 82

CHAPTER 8: FOUNDATION OF SPECIAL STRENGTH 85
Strength Speed 85
Shock Method 86
Pulling Shock Methods 87
    Weightlifting Style Pulls 88
    Special Squats for Shock Methods 89
    Pressing Shock Methods 90
    OTHER SHOCK METHODS 91
    Maximal Eccentrics 91
    Overspeed Eccentrics 91
    Maximum Eccentrics 91
    Forced Repetition 92
RESTRICTED RANGE POWER BACK WORK 92
Isometric Strength 92
    The Advantages of Isometrics 93
    Isometric Disadvantages 94
Reactive Methods 94
Combination Resistance Methods 94
Heavy-Light System for Explosive Power 95
    Results of an 18-month Experiment 95
The Combination for Explosive Strength 96

CHAPTER 9: CIRCA MAX CHART 111
Other Methods, Accentuation 111
Peak-Contraction Principle 112

CHAPTER 10: CONJUGATE SYSTEM OF TRAINING 113

CHAPTER 11: SPEED STRENGTH 115
Compensatory Acceleration Training or CAT 117

CHAPTER 12: STATIC DYNAMIC DEVELOPMENT 119
Proven Methods Of Strength Development 121
    Maximal Effort Method 121
    Dynamic Effort Method 122
    Repeated Effort Method 122
    The Plan 123
Reduce Running And Add The Right Strength Training 124
    Explosive-Strength Training 124
    Belt Squat Machine 125
    Hamstring Work 125
    Hamstring Maintenance 126
    Plyometric Swing 126
    Non-Motorized Treadmill 126
    Static Dynamic Developer 127
More Equipment 127
    Bars 127
    Sleds 128
The Speed Barrier 128

CHAPTER 13: PULLING EXERCISES 131
Deadlifting for Explosive Power 134
Olympic Style Workouts 136
    Speed Strength 137

CHAPTER 14: SPECIAL SURFACE JUMPING 139
    The Method 139

CHAPTER 15: TIME RELATED DISTANCE WORKOUTS 143

CHAPTER 16: SPECIAL WEIGHT TRAINING FOR LONG DISTANCE ... 149
The Safety Squat Bar 150
The Sled 151
The Wheelbarrow Push or Pull 151
The Belt Squat Machine 151
The Maximal Effort Method 153
The Dynamic Method 153
The Repeated/Repetition Method 153
The Use of Exercises 153

CHAPTER 17: THE SPEED BARRIER ... 155
Restoration For Sprinters ... 156
Reactive Methods Plus Contrast Methods ... 158
Special Strength Development ... 159
Bad Examples ... 161

CHAPTER 18: JAMAICAN SECRETS OR SYSTEM? ... 167
What are the facts? ... 167
What is, and How to Use, Accommodation Resistance ... 169

CHAPTER 19: WEIGHT PROGRAMS ... 173
Three Week Pendulum Waves ... 173
Speed Strength ... 175
Maximal Method ... 176
Methods Not Recommended ... 178

SUMMING UP ... 179

SELECTED BIBLIOGRAPHY & REFERENCES ... 183

ACKNOWLEDGEMENT

The knowledge of special strength training and periodization plus realizing the need to stimulate training programs by adding the new volume, intensities, exercises or personal into the training environment none of this could be possible without naming just a few soviet lifters, coaches, and sports scientists. They include A D Ermakov, V. M. Zatsiorsky, N.S. Atanasov, Y.V. Verkhoshansky, V.I. Frolov, B. Tabachnik, Arosiev, R. Roman, N. Romanov, N. Ozolin, B. Ross, H.B. Paschall, T. Starzynski, A.N. Medvedev, H. Sozanski, P. Komi, A. V. Hill, C. Bosco, A. Bondarchuk, R. Berger, L. Abadjiev, A.S. Prilepin

And special thanks to Mel Siff of Supertraining Fame. You understand what westside was doing and helped me to further understand sports science.

PREFACE

This book is intended for coaches to develop strength and power the correct way. It may appear like many books by Westside, but it is completely designed for running any distance. It is a collection of 35 years of discovering the best methods to build strength and improve power. Some methods are complex while others are very simple, but proven by time. This book will explain problems that may have held your training methods back.

A running coach should train not only technique but also strength and power. Furthermore, learn how to train optimally, and prevent most injuries.

"The wisest man has something yet to learn." – George Santayana.

CHAPTER 1

Introduction: Learning What an Athlete Needs

The major idea of this training book is not to completely understand how to build all special strength, but rather to learn what an athlete needs. Earning an exercise science degree will seldom bring the coach closer to solving the athlete's training problems. It takes decades of non-stop work and countless experiments to build an effective system that encompasses all aspects of training.

Too Many Injuries

There are far too many injuries in track. They seem to be so common that many think they must be a part of the routine. The author trained one athlete that for the six previous years was constantly hampered by lower body injuries. After training at Westside for nine weeks and establishing new records, including the first race of the year, they were totally amazed. And so was the author at the mere thought of someone expecting to be injured as part of the training protocol.

The injuries come from over exertion of the lower body limbs. This is due to too much running, which is one of the most stressful activities one endures. Running too much also leads to the so-called speed barrier. Sozanski states there are two methods to overcome a speed barrier. One method is to simply encourage the athlete to run faster. This should always be the case between the coach and athlete, plus the athlete's training partners. The other method called for by experts such as Romanola is running on an inclined track or a descending start. A caution—this method can distort normal running technique. Even with that caution, the author finds the second far superior to the first. When one covers a predetermined distance—say 100 meters, 200 meters, 800 meters or 1600 meters—one finds himself or herself running the same times for the same race. The distance will never change, but the time must change or no further progress will be realized. After mastering proper running form, only by adding more strength and power will one's times get better.

Getting Better

Getting better, stronger and faster can be done two ways. First, doing general exercises will help increase technical skills and other abilities by raising a lagging muscle group such as hamstrings, calves, or hip and glute muscles. The exercises can be directed to a muscle group by doing special exercises or covering a distance for times with several forms of resistance such as a weight sled, ankle weights, weight vest, or bars. No one can cover the same distance with resistance at the same time, but rather track all-times with resistance. An example would be covering 400m with a 45-pound weight sled that will take from two minutes 15 seconds to possibly three minutes. As the times are reduced, the athlete is producing more force production that will make it possible to run faster when the form of resistance is removed.

Speed of movement can be increased by the contrast method where one trains with resistance, then removes the resistance. The faster speed is due to the increased excitability of the central nervous system (CNS) provided by the movement with extra resistance. Even when reduced, the extra resistance remains present in the mind of the athlete. While at the same time, the resistance builds all the running muscles along with adding to muscle recovery. That technique is much less stressful on the athlete's body. It also prevents boredom. Instead of having one distance and one top time, the athlete can now have many time records to break. This is the conjugate system at work aiding in recovery.

Overuse injuries, overuse injuries, overuse injuries—the author hears this over and over. This is insane to say the least, or better known by science as the law of accommodation. This simply means when the athlete repeats the same exercises, volume, and intensity their progress will stop and many times go backward.

You can avoid accommodation by switching exercises and the total volume, as well as the intensity zones, and by constantly rotating the special exercises as well as reducing the amount of running. Running too much leads to overuse injuries that are repeated every season. There are two words that must be used by the coach that leads to recovery—optimal and restoration. Experts like Zalesky (1979) refer to phases of recovery.

Recovery

On-going recovery is best utilized by constantly rotating special exercises or altering the volume or intensity of the work. Read the periodization section (Page 10) very carefully. This is part of the conjugate system.

This system allows one to train speed, strength, and endurance all at the same time by unidirectional means. While many have had small success with this method, Westside relies on it totally. The greater the athlete, the greater the stimulus must be to raise the level of preparedness. By rotating special weight and jumping exercises, it works as on-going recovery. This aids in recovery from workout to workout.

A second method of recovery is rapid recovery. This happens immediately after a workout. This can mean anything from taking a shower, to simply taking a nap, to meditation or playing your favorite music. One can take a supplement that is intended for recovery. To reach the top in track and field training, the total volume must be raised over the years so recovery must play a role in training. There are many things that can be affected by an over-training effect. Heart rate, sleep patterns, breathing patterns, concentration, a lower pain threshold, and even general irritability and alertness just to name a few things for the coach to monitor. Many times the coach totally neglects these signs. Many times a specialist or a therapist must be enlisted.

The third and last recovery method is the conjugate system of constantly rotating exercises. The exercises work primary muscles that are accounted for in most of running. Add to the rotation the use of a three-week pendulum wave for maintaining total volume through rising, then lowering, the intensity zone. Changing special exercises just before totally adapting to them will constantly stimulate athlete growth. As Ben Tabachnik said, "To adapt to training is to never fully adapt to training." Most track careers are cut in half by overuse injuries. This can be resolved by constantly using new training stimulus.

Use New Improved Training Methods

There is more than one way to train a runner of any distance and it is a better way. New workouts can relieve stress and boredom. If you are using the same training methods for the past 20 years, you are most likely 20 years behind. The Westside system is based on having different groups use different training means to analyze which group makes the most progress. The track athlete must seek out an expert weight training coach or do an internship under one that is directed toward sprinting and running of all distances. Work closely with experts of restoration and recovery and the psychological aspects of training and competition as well. Leave any facet out of the plan and you fail.

CHAPTER 2

Fundamentals to Contemplate

We know that walking and running are both cyclic movements, as both have consecutive strides.

Walking is when one foot is always touching the ground. Running is when the ground contact is broken, which is known as the non-supporting phase. Dr. Romanoff, Bud Winter and Barry Ross, along with many others, talk about the importance of the support leg in relation to the body's center of gravity, or CG. This is most important for vertical movements.

Make a checklist of a sprint. Let's first look at reaction time. This can be done by recording the time between the firing of the starting gun to the very first muscular reaction of the sprinter. Reaction time can be thought of as quickness. This is the ability of the CNS to contract, relax, or control muscle function without any preliminary stretch. According to *Supertraining*, it is measured as a time interval between stimulus and response. It can be increased by jumping and bounding. After receiving the signal from the CNS, by noise or touch, this reaction time can be one percent.

There is a chart in a fine book by Bud Winter and Jimson Lee, entitled *The Rocket Sprint Start*, which informs the reader of each phase of the race and what percentage it takes to cover that phase. The author takes it as how much training time the model athlete must spend on each phase. Therefore, if Bud Winter says that 60 percent to 65 percent of a 100-meter race is acceleration, then 65 percent of one's training should be allotted towards acceleration. It is that simple.

But, performing countless sprints of any distance will not do it, rather more strength and power will. This must be done through many different methods. It is likely that the track coach will lack a great knowledge of strength and power training, and therefore often will just repeat the same programming over and over again. The author has repeatedly used the word accommodation. When one continuously uses the same training loads, volume, and exercises, or even the same rest intervals, performance will decrease. This is a general law of biology. More on this can be found in *The Science and Practice of Strength Training* by V. M. Zatsiorsky.

Anyone can make progress in the beginning, as a novice. An advanced athlete, however, needs advanced methods. *Supertraining* by Mel Siff takes it a step further. Using the same method, volumes, and intensity, once again, will result in accommodation. There are four sectors of training in this manner: adaptation, habituation, stagnation, and deterioration.

To avoid this, use the Westside Conjugate System explained throughout this book.

Now, let's look at the acceleration phase and what it requires. **What is a sprint?** The definition of a sprint is to run or go at top speed, especially for a short distance. **What is biomechanics?** Biomechanics is the study of the mechanics of a living body, especially of the forces exerted by the muscles and gravity on the skeletal structure. There is constant talk about running biomechanics, always looking for running perfection. One key to success for Usain Bolt was fewer strides. Bolt uses 41 strides while most top sprinters take 43 to 48, making the average 45. Bolt also weighs more than his competitors; therefore he must be much stronger and more powerful to be able to perform fewer strides. Also, his stride gives him an advantage over all others. They say he can run even faster than 9.58 with better technique; Although, you could say that about any sprinter. There are too many experts on this subject.

Michael Johnson, the 400-meter world record holder, also has flaws in his form. Yet, these two men hold the 100-150, 200, 300, and 400-meter records. How do they do it without perfect form? They must produce a greater force on the support foot. Many claim ground force depends partially on your technique, but mostly on how much strength your leg muscles can generate. (Note: there are 1,000 to one running mechanics to real knowledgeable strength and power coaches. This is a problem.)

Technique is essential, but how strong the correct muscles are is far more important. One must consider that very strong muscles can ensure very good technique. Remember, how strong not how big. This calls for the correct muscle types. Type II B is the maximal force production fibers. They are not only the largest, but also have the highest potential for increasing size and strength. They are, of course, what all top sprinters and weightlifters are comprised of.

Mass-specific force, or MSF, is a term Barry Ross uses to describe the body weight strength ratio of an athlete. Adding weight, but not strength, can reduce MSF. But if proper weight training is done, it is possible to become more powerful while maturing and adding bodyweight. For example, Shalon, a 17-year-old girl, started at Westside with a 36-inch box jump. Her bodyweight then was 137 pounds. As her strength increased substantially, her bodyweight also increased to 147 pounds, but now with faster times and a 50 $1/_2$-inch box jump record. Shalon received a full-ride college scholarship to run track. At the end of her first season, her times were slower than they were in high school and her bodyweight was up to 157 pounds. Indeed, her MSF went down. Upon returning to Westside after her freshman year of college, her box jump was at 42 inches. Why? She experienced a gain in body weight, was doing no box jumps, and had a lack of power. Her coach had told her she lacked elastic energy. Of course she did. The coach never had her perform box jumps, and she had gained weight. After one three-week wave at Westside, and at a bodyweight of 159 pounds, she tested out a 53 $1/_2$-inch box jump record. How? We used a three-week wave for speed strength, with 50 to 60 percent bar weight, plus 25 percent band tension, at a bar speed of roughly .8-.9$^{m/}_{s}$ for acceleration. Then, we added explosive strength training with 30 percent bar weight, plus 25 percent band tension. For speed strength, she performed 25 lifts per week and 40 explosive squats along with 80 weighted jumps.

The shock method is used on Max Effort (ME) day. It is rotated each week with a different barbell exercise. For example, a rack pull, concentric squat, power clean, or forced reps. Yes, there are many methods of shock training besides depth jumps, which can be very dangerous. We know an advanced male sprinter can produce 1,000 pounds per step. The average is 44 per 100 meters, which adds up to 44,000 pounds of work in 10 seconds. Let's say a female sprinter can produce 500 pounds per step and takes 50 steps per 100 meters. That adds up to 25,000 pounds of work in 11 seconds. The work load of a 1,000-pound squatter at Westside is 12,000 pounds in one workout that takes 15 minutes while wearing protective shorts. Now, it becomes very clear why there are so many leg and hip injuries in track. Track athletes have very little or no base of strength training throughout the season. Remember that the 1,000-pound squatter does 60,000 pounds of reverse hypers in two workouts and 20,000 pounds on two more for restoration, plus banded leg curls, glute-ham raises, and other assorted posterior chain work. After all, Usain Bolt is larger than most sprinters and most produce more strength and power to carry a load faster than anyone else in the world.

Remember MSF (mass-specific force)? Do you understand now why it is of importance to avoid block periodization as it becomes a detraining program? Again, 90 percent of the effort to run down a track is horizontal, or to overcome gravity. Why are our squats done on a box? Squats are done on a box because running involves a fast change of muscular contraction and relaxation. This, like box squatting, breaks up the eccentric and concentric phases for greater muscle ligament and tendon elasticity.

Speaking of elasticity of the muscles and tendons, they play a large role in increasing the motor output in sports movements. The elasticity is stored in the muscle or tendon when stretched. This causes deformation energy during the support phase, meaning ground contact. Think of a basketball as it is dropped to the floor, the bottom will flatten out to some extent. This is called deformation. This also happens to the plantar flexors of the foot as it is stretched during the first part of the support periods, and then shortened afterward. Remember the basketball? And how when it bounces off of the ground it will flatten to some extent? Now, throw it down as hard as possible and see how much deformation it sustains, meaning how flat it became on the downward phase just to return to its original shape. The faster the ball is thrown down, the higher it will bounce upwards. This is proven in Hooke's Law of Elasticity. The foot speed while touching the ground is not a perfect collision where no KE is lost, but rather, not perfectly elastic either due to having less KE after touching the ground.

There is a virtual force occurring during the support phase. Virtual force is a force that is present, but not recognized. One can walk on ice, but cannot jump on ice or it will break. This is a virtual force. This force causes far too many injuries in running. Remember, a top sprinter is producing 1,000 pounds per step. How? Through overspeed eccentrics! Often a track coach was once a sprinter themselves with constant running with pain in the calves and shins or hamstrings from too much running. But, somehow, once they become a coach and sit behind the desk, they forget what they went through and force their team to repeat the same mismanagement of training that they also endured. Why? The hardest thing a person can do is change. But, they must change for the bettering of their athletes. More is not better, a smarter plan is. There are too many injuries in sprinting as well as all distance running, but I can't see anything being done to prevent them.

Westside Barbell has a reputation for not ever having tendonitis problems, regardless of the massive weights lifted and the extreme volume in a weekly, monthly, and yearly plan. Why? Westside performs countless lightweight repetitions for the joints and sole tissue. For example, 200 leg curls each day, rotating from ankle weight curls, standing leg curls, band curls, and inverse leg curls. Six hundred glute-ham raises per month for hamstring maintenance. Walking with a wheelbarrow forward and backward as well as walking or jogging a slow run with a safety squat bar for 400 meters. This work is constantly rotated at least once per week to avoid accommodation. Most athletes at Westside under 200 pounds will also jump rope. A program for a sprinter with the capability of a 400-pound squat will consist of 20,000 pounds of reverse hypers two times per week, and two workouts of 10,000 pounds of reverse hypers. That is 60,000 pounds of direct work for the hamstrings, hips, glutes, and low back, with no compression of the spine. This work is in an open chain setting, meaning with no opposing forces of gravity on the athlete. Walk in a belt squat machine for three minutes. Walks will build all the lower body muscles for running without compression of the spine.

This is not just harder training, but also smarter training. Why run ten 200 meters when most races have, at most, two heats and a final? This is not an exercise specificity. It is just overtraining and making the sprinter slower as they will conserve themselves, even without knowing, just to finish the workout. Running the same distance over and over again will only cause a speed barrier. In the book, *The Science of Sports Training*, Thomas Kurz states that by doing the same training regiment, meaning the same reps, time intervals, and exercises in an attempt to improve an event, one will not improve. Rather, they will learn to run at a certain speed and not any faster due to their physical abilities such as reaction time, mobility, flexibility, or a special strength. This is the speed barrier. The author believes the speed barrier occurs in training by having a first-year student do the same program for the next four years of high school or college. Each year, the training must be more difficult. We know that within 10 to 14 days, one will lose strength and more importantly speed, if not trained. A 1999 study by Sozanski, Witczak, and Starzynski found that if one replaces sport-specific speed exercises with directed and general speed and strength exercises, it is possible to increase the runner's sport-specific speed. This is what the Conjugate System does at Westside. Using an array of special exercises to improve a specific sport's speed at a later date is referred to as delayed transmutation.

Delayed Transmutation

Although this system of training refers to not doing the actual event, the author suggests doing an exercise that is similar to the event. This could mean a snatch or a full sprint. For example, substituting many forms of special strength pulls, as well as small special exercises that contribute to the snatch, such as things like back extensions, glute-ham raises, and shrugs. For sprinting, consider lots of jumping, power sled walks with heavy weight for top speed maintenance, and lightweight sled sprinting with 10 kilograms for women and 20 kilograms for men, mostly in the grass to reduce the stress on the lower legs.

This training is much higher in total volume and intensity. Then, reduce the work, for a so-called tapering phase during the delayed transformation phase, which is designed to reach the athletes full potential at meet time. This process happens best when an all-out workout is performed 21 days out from the event. Reduce the effort to 75 percent of the all-out workout 14 days before the biggest event(s). Then, include even more tapering, to roughly 50 percent of the work performed 21 days out. This is delayed transformation, making it possible to reach the athlete's full potential when it counts, meet day. This is what setting up the correct periodization plan can do.

CHAPTER 3

Periodization—Division Into Training Periods

I knew Western periodization was a dead-end as early as 1973, which was the year I broke my back for the first time, but I knew no other way. In 1981 after breaking my L5 the second time, I had to find a better way. I would be strong in one lift, but not the other two. It would be a different lift that would go up while some other lifts were unmanageable. Ricky Crain, a great lifter, would call me with the same story. Dave Waddington, the first 1,000-pound squatter was in my living room and asked how to fix the same problem Ricky and I had. I told him to call me when he found the answer.

So back to 1981, I was desperate. I made a call to Bud Charniga to buy some Soviet books on training. He said, "Lou, you know these are like textbooks written by their Sports scientists on very intricate matters on training." I told Bud that is exactly what I needed because the Western gradual overload system led me down a dead-end road. It is more of a de-training system than anything else. But, enough talking about the past …

Three-Week Speed Strength Waves

I looked at the models of Matveyev, his wave system, and the wave-like concentration of loading for five to eight weeks at a time by Verkhoshansky. I then looked at the pendulum approach by Arosiev, which is used for alternating special strength preparation such as speed strength, explosive strength, strength speed and even strength endurance. I also looked at Tudor O. Bompa, Ph.D., and his findings. It was interesting to me how effective the system was that made Naim Suleymanoglu the great Bulgarian weightlifter. I realized the system was for a model athlete or someone of perfect proportion for his sport. It was based on the hypothesis of Felix Meerson (Plasticeskoe Obezpecenie Organizma, 1967) and Hiden's findings from 1960 to 1964.

Which one was the best, or was there a best? These were, after all, very intelligent men, to say the least. I had found before that; however, I did not like a long-term plan. I discovered in my training and my training plateaus that after going upward for three weeks, I would regress almost every time. I like the wave system of training by Matveyev and Verkhoshansky, but Vorobyev's (1978) wave plan was a little less restrictive, somewhat like Ermakov's work in 1974.

Dr. Siff asked me how I came up with a three-week speed strength wave. I told him I became no stronger or faster after three weeks, and he was fascinated to hear that because V. Alexez, the great Soviet SHW lifter, used the same three-week wave. On week four, he re-evaluated the training and started a new three-week wave cycle. I think I won Mel Siff over at that point.

There are some different approaches I implement, and I seldom do a regular squat or deadlift. As the meet approaches, we don't reduce special exercises but push them to the limit to perfect form by concentrating on the weak muscle group. This is what the conjugate system does. There are three phases that are strength training: Maximal Effort, Dynamic Method, and Repetition Method for hypertrophy, which are all trained simultaneously. There is built-in flexibility in a three-week pendulum wave.

Volume and Intensity Zones

The first graphs concerning volume and intensity zones also show the importance of waving the volume and percentage of a one rep max again to avoid accommodation. The speed strength days show high volume and moderate to low intensity. On max effort days, the opposite will and must occur. The volume is 35 percent to 50 percent of the speed days, but as the intensities must be as high as possible, hopefully, a new all-time record will be set. Like the Bulgarians, the level of preparedness is the major factor for how much one can lift on max effort day.

Figure 1.1. Low volume training; highest intensity possible for 100 percent and above. Limit to three lifts of 90 percent and above.

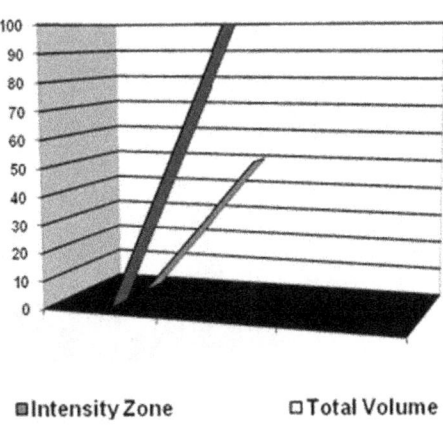

Figure 1.2. High volume training; moderate intensity zones between 60 percent to 85 percent. Limit to 12 to 24 lifts per training session.

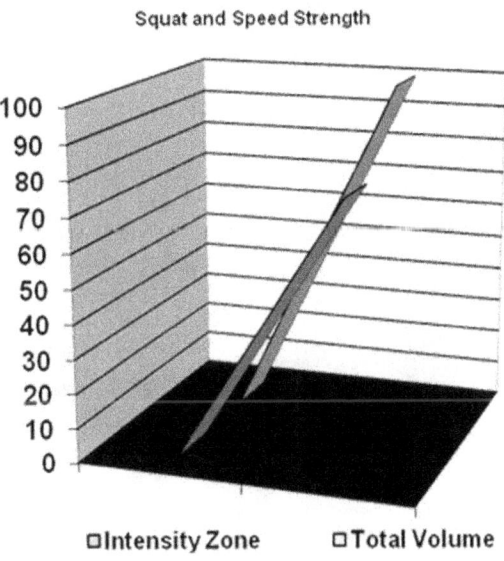

*Figure 1.3. High-volume training; **low to moderate intensity**; between 50 percent to 60 percent. Limit 16 to 30 lifts per training session.*

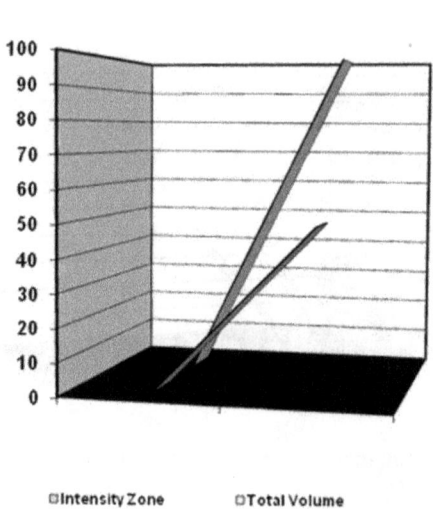

Figure 1.4. Low-volume training; highest intensity possible. Limit to three lifts of 90 percent and above.

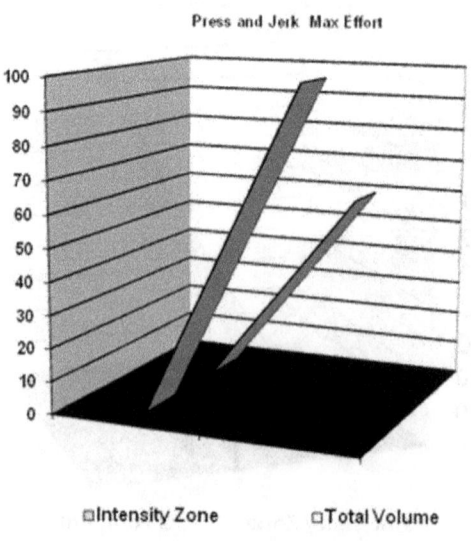

Four Direct Periods of Periodization

1. **Accumulation**—high volume training of all types to charge or build the body for speed or strength for a particular sport.

2. **Intensification**—now the athlete limits to some degree the exercises concentrating on more specific speed work or strength movements that work best for him or her.

3. **Transformation**—now the value of the previous two cycles is to test while the athlete uses exercises that are most beneficial to the competition. For lifting, the top lifter uses a circa-max or near-max weight phase with limited special exercise that contribute to his or her highest achievements. A runner's work would be very limited to the very most important speed or speed endurance work.

4. **Delayed Transformation**—here, one reduces the high-intensity work and relies on rest and restoration for two to four weeks leading up to a competition. We found that 21 days is best for the heaviest training weight. We then taper down to meet time.

It is imperative to know about these phases of training. Refer to the suggested reading for more information on periodization.

THE IMPORTANCE OF OBSERVATION

During the Westside system of using a three-week wave for speed strength and explosive speed training, the wave rotates from 75 percent to 85 percent in a three-week cycle, jumping five percent per week. By doing this, I can evaluate the progress of the athlete all the time. This makes more sense to observe the athlete to see if he or she has become stronger or faster as well as other physical qualities such as quickness or where muscle mass should be added. I don't have a crystal ball, so I have no idea where the athlete's progress will be in 12 weeks or 24 weeks. The three-week wave system allows for better observation on a continuous basis. For maximal effort work each week the major barbell exercises are changed.

ELIMINATING ACCOMMODATION

Soviet sports scientists found after three weeks of weight training at 90 percent or more, progress stopped. This is accommodation, but it is eliminated by revolving the barbell exercises each week. We can max out every week throughout the year, and extreme workouts can occur every 72 hours. Our weekly plan is to speed squat on Friday with high volume of 75 percent to 85 percent intensity zone for three reps per set. On Monday it is max effort work for squatting or pulling for max singles. The intensity is 100 percent plus all an individual can do on that particular day similar to the Bulgarian system. No more than three lifts from 90 percent up to a new max. Of course, the volume is low much like the Rule of 60 percent. Speed press and jerks on Sunday; High volume and very low intensity zones range from 40 percent to 50 percent. Wednesday is max effort day, working up to a new personal record or as much as possible. Do this with single lifts not more than three lifts at 90 percent, approaching 100 percent; plus, in one week the speed work is 20 to 30 lifts while the max effort day is three lifts. It is almost a 10 to 1 ratio with speed lifts beginning the 10, and max lifts being 1.

The bulk of our system is special exercises. We do not have a system to form a model athlete, so it may take several combinations of special exercises to make one succeed. Our entire training program is built around special exercises for weightlifting, powerlifting or running and jumping. I don't concentrate on what you have, but rather what you don't have.

An NFL agent brought in a lineman and asked me what I was going to do. I told him, and he said, "Why aren't you going to run him?" I asked him this question, "He ran for four years and this is how fast he is. Why do you think two more months of running with him will make a difference?" He replied, "Good point."

Nine-Week Training Cycle

Let's look at pendulum waves with special bars. The graphs show a nine-week training cycle, consisting of three different three-week pendulum waves. The nine-week system employs three types of bars. They each have a maximum weight to calculate the percentage. All three maximums are different to avoid the mistake of accommodation or using the same volume repeatedly. The bar path will be somewhat different as well to ensure training all leg and back muscles. The bar speed by percents will be close, but the bar weight is quite different.

Figure 2.1. This graph shows bar weight for weeks one through three.

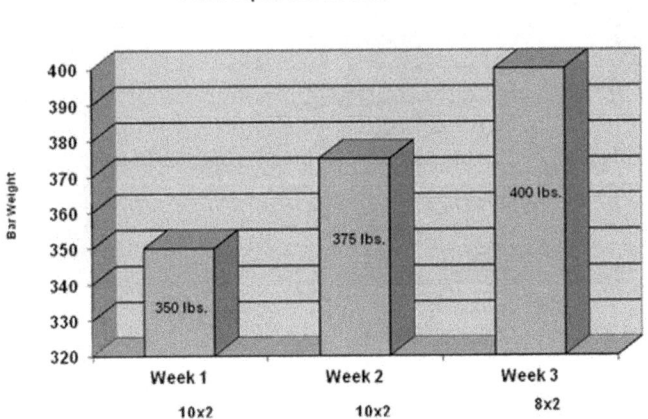

Figure 2.2. This graph shows volume for weeks one through three.

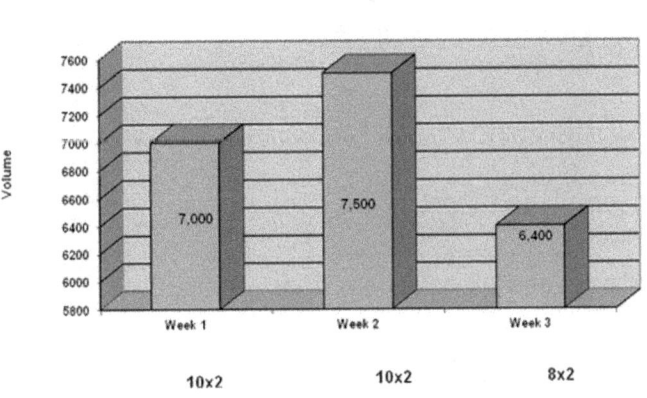

Figure 2.3. This graph shows percentages for weeks one through three.

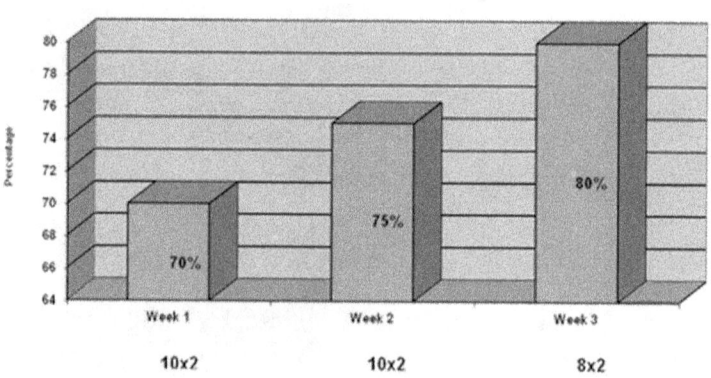

Figure 2.4. This graph shows bar weight for weeks four through six.

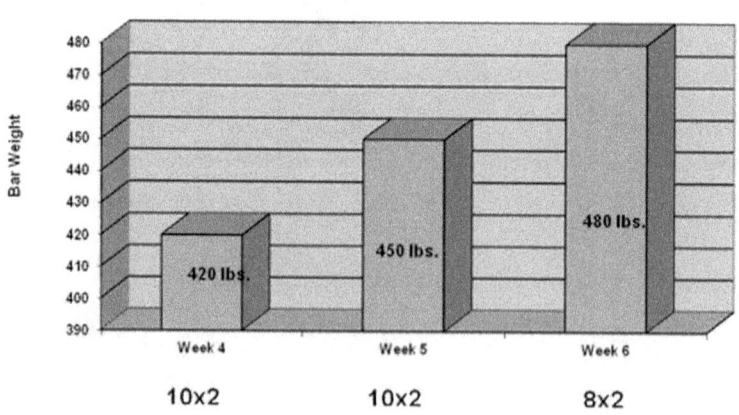

Figure 2.5. This graph shows volume for weeks four through six.

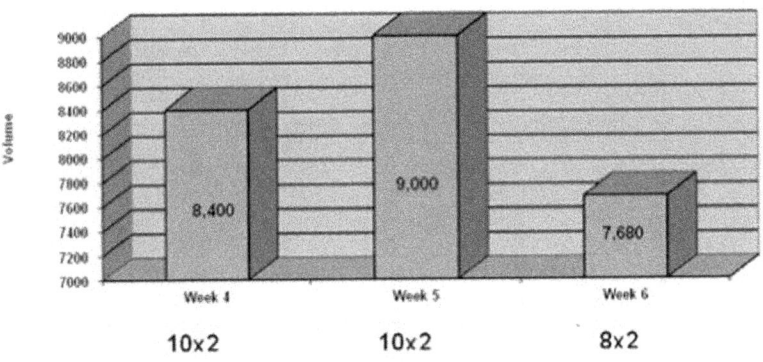

Figure 2.6. This graph shows percentages for weeks four through six.

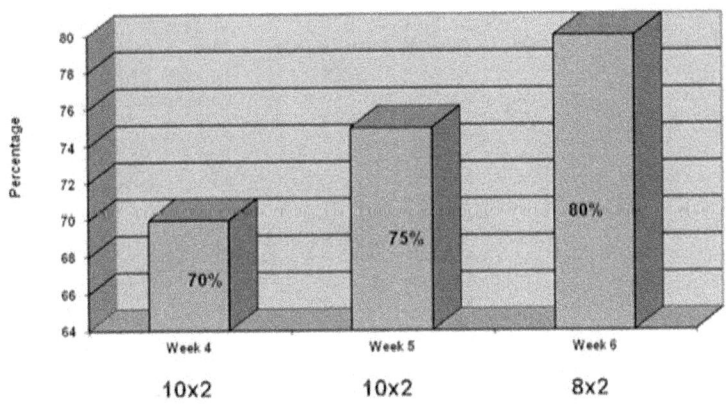

Figure 2.7. This graph shows bar weight for weeks seven through nine.

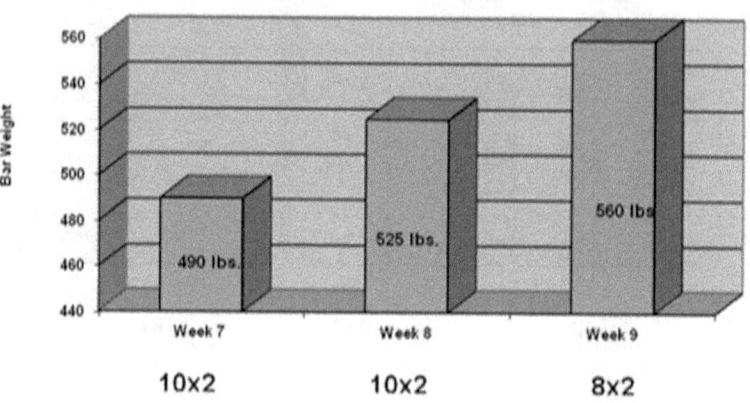

Figure 2.8. This graph shows volume for weeks seven through nine.

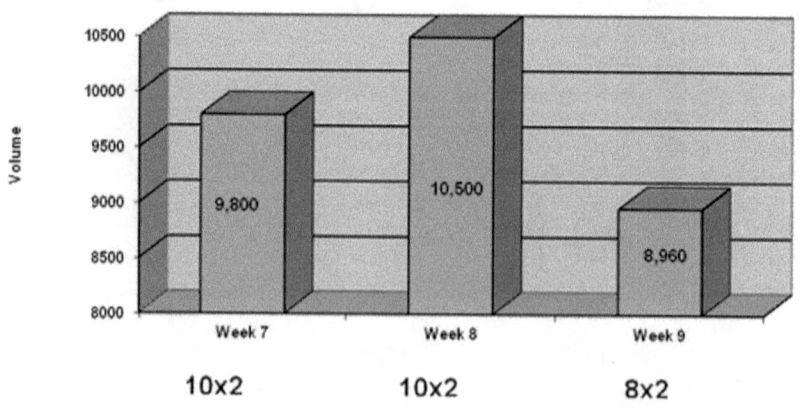

Figure 2.9. This graph shows percentages for weeks seven through nine.

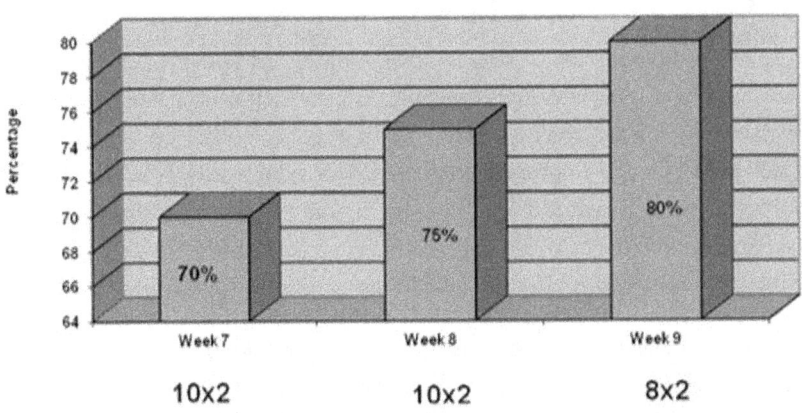

More Wave Cycle Discussion

The wave cycles vary as bands, chains, or combinations of both are added to the barbell to accommodate resistance. When using weight releasers, the added weight on the first eccentric repetition phase can be calculated. The variations of a wave are too numerous to list.

The speed strength waves for squatting, jerk, and press normally last three weeks, and the strength speed waves last only two weeks due to their severity as well as the near max or circa-max wave phases. If the speed day waves are of ultra-high volume for squatting with speed pulls following, the squats are also of high volume workout. A speed strength squat day is followed by a maximal effort day 72 hours later; then, a high volume squat and deadlift follows 72 hours afterwards, then they de-load. Most can only sustain three max effort workouts in a row. On de-load day, work on special exercises or form.

The next scheduled max effort is replaced by a Repetition Method workout to recover from the severity of such training. Then, embark on as heavy a workload for three or four more workouts. For the squat and pull, this approach works for the pressing days as well, such as standing press or some form of bench pressing at or angled. Remember when you feel mentally or physically exhausted, replace the normal speed or max effort workouts with a repetition workout designed for working the less fatigued muscle groups. Repetition work means lots of extensions for the back, hips, arms and trunk.

Note to reader: Speed strength cycles last two or three weeks progressively, going higher in percentage and somewhat higher volume. On max effort days, the barbell exercise must change each week. Example: One week is a squat exercise, a pulling exercise the next, followed by a Goodmorning exercise and occasionally, a repetition day thrown in for recovery for overtaxed muscles. These are in no particular order. Exercises must be chosen for individual goals. Again, repetition work must consist of single joint exercises. Example exercises are back raises, glute/ham raises, tricep extensions, and the like.

Unlike many athletes who have a yearly or even a multi-year plan or the plan and methodology for an Olympic cycle, it is planned with a timetable for developing certain systems. Their concept is to increase intensity while lowering volume, making a functional plan on how fast an individual will be, how high he can jump, or how much he can lift at a particular date during the year. Then and only then will progress be noted. Is the athlete ahead or behind schedule?

Monitoring Progress with the Westside System

The Westside System of training can check speed strength every week. This is done with the three-week pendulum wave. Explosive strength can be monitored the same as jumping progress. Maximal strength for upper and lower body is monitored each week. Potential new personal records (PRs) can be done at over 90 percent, sometimes 95 percent, year-long. Remember to note the four periods of training—accumulation, intensification, transformation and delayed transformation—are used only in the beginning of training. Then, all aspects are combined simultaneously through a yearly plan.

The Westside System prepares the athlete for the delayed transformation period or the circa-max phase that Westside uses for power meets. It is a wave of the highest intensity; hopefully, a new record of some type is set, depending on the sport. The critical delayed transformation phase or the de-loading phase trains from explosive to maximal strength, covering all elements of strength: coordination, fitness, flexibility, raising lactic acid, aerobic and anaerobic, threshold barriers while increasing VO2 max. All components can and must be trained simultaneously. Delayed transformation was adapted from track and field, and from Olympic weightlifters from the former Soviet Union.

Periodization can be a weekly, monthly or yearly plan. This plan can lead to a four-year or an Olympic cycle. Speaking of Olympic cycles, a college athlete's sports career can be four years for improving leg and back strength, and there must be a mathematical system to follow. Westside has used the wave system of periodization for more than 30 years with great success. It is, of course, a math problem to be addressed that combines bar speed, total volume and precise intensity zones of a predetermined percent of a one rep max. This along with proper biomechanics and physics can spell certain success. One such plan is outlined next.

The Plan: From a 400- to a 1,000-Pound Squat 400-Pound Max Squat

400-Pound Max Squat

Percent	Weight (pounds)	Reps	Lifts	Band Tension	Volume
50%	200	12x2	24	25%	4,800 lb
55%	220	12x2	24	25%	5,280 lb
60%	240	10x2	20	25%	4,800 lb
Bar Speed is 0.8 m/s avg.					

450-Pound Max Squat

Percent	Weight (pounds)	Reps	Lifts	Band Tension	Volume
50%	225	12x2	24	25%	5,400 lb
55%	250	12x2	24	25%	6,000 lb
60%	270	10x2	20	25%	5,400 lb
Bar Speed is 0.8 m/s avg.					

500-Pound Max Squat

Percent	Weight (pounds)	Reps	Lifts	Band Tension	Volume
50%	250	12x2	24	25%	6,000 lb
55%	275	12x2	24	25%	6,600 lb
60%	300	10x2	20	25%	6,000 lb
Bar Speed is 0.8 m/s avg.					

550-Pound Max Squat

Percent	Weight (pounds)	Reps	Lifts	Band Tension	Volume
50%	275	12x2	24	25%	6,600 lb
55%	300	12x2	24	25%	7,200 lb
60%	330	10x2	20	25%	6,600 lb
Bar Speed is 0.8 m/s avg.					

600-Pound Max Squat

Percent	Weight (pounds)	Reps	Lifts	Band Tension	Volume
50%	300	12x2	24	25%	7,200 lb
55%	330	12x2	24	25%	7,920 lb
60%	360	10x2	20	25%	7,200 lb
Bar Speed is 0.8 m/s avg.					

650-Pound Max Squat

Percent	Weight (pounds)	Reps	Lifts	Band Tension	Volume
50%	325	12x2	24	25%	7,800 lb
55%	355	12x2	24	25%	8,520 lb
60%	390	10x2	20	25%	7,800 lb
Bar Speed is 0.8 m/s avg.					

700-Pound Max Squat

Percent	Weight (pounds)	Reps	Lifts	Band Tension	Volume
50%	350	12x2	24	25%	8,400 lb
55%	385	12x2	24	25%	9,240 lb
60%	420	10x2	20	25%	8,400 lb
Bar Speed is 0.8 m/s avg.					

Notice the bar speed is constant, roughly .8 m/s. Also note that it requires a total of 600 pounds of volume to increase the squat 50 pounds, and the percent range is 50 percent to 60 percent. The rep range and the total number of lifts remain the same. The amount of band tension or chains is also constant. The three-week waves for a period of time yields the 50-pound increase by building maximal strength on max effort day, 72 hours later plus special exercises.

By studying these graphs carefully, it can be seen how mathematics plays a large role in gaining strength and force production.

Let's look at the total volume for a 400-pound max squat. It is one-half of the total volume of an 800-pound max squat. A 400-pound max squat requires one to maintain 4,800 pounds of volume; whereas, 800 pounds involves 9,600 pounds of volume. This is twice as much as a 400-pound squat. A 500-pound squatter must maintain 6,000 pounds of volume. It takes 12,000 pounds to maintain a 1,000-pound squat, which is exactly twice the volume. While the goal as a coach may be to maintain a squat max of 400 pounds or 700 pounds for a lineman to be able to ensure the force development of the before-mentioned squat, the appropriate volume must be adhered to. This is a proven method of strength training, which is referred to as the Dynamic Method.

The primary goal is to develop a fast rate of force development in sports of all kinds. For those who use a Tendo unit, speed strength is the goal of 0.8 to 0.9 m/s average. Speed strength is trained at intermediate velocities. Know what velocity a particular special strength is trained at or failure will ensue while attempting to improve a special strength. These speeds can be found on Page 150 in Mel Siff's *Supertraining*, 2003.

To avoid accommodation in volume in a weekly plan, the special exercises will fluctuate to such an extent that accommodation is impossible. A second method is to change the total volume while training at a certain percent while using a three-week wave and a cycle is to use a special bar at the same percent. The workload can change. It is evident that a particular percent—this time 50 percent—can greatly change the work load when doing a back squat compared to a front squat or an overhead squat. The example shows that a typical 500-pound back squatter would normally have a max front squat of 350 pounds and an overhead squat of an estimated 250 pounds. When looking at the first week wave at 50 percent in the three different squat styles, the total volume per set of two reps would be respectively 500 pounds, 350 pounds, and 250 pounds.

Changing Volume While Maintaining Bar Speed

Max	Percent	Weight (pounds)	Volume
500 lb back squat	50%	250	500 lb per set
350 lb front squat	50%	175	350 lb per set
250 lb overhead squat	50%	125	250 lb per set

This is the simplest way to change volume while maintaining bar speed at the predetermined bar speed at the fixed weekly percent. For more examples, the three graphs below show using chains for a 400-pound max squat; a 600-pound max squat, and an 800-pound max squat. For benching, the bar weight remains the same, but the accommodating resistance changes accordingly as maximum strength goes up.

BAND JERK AND PRESS WORKOUT FOR SPEED STRENGTH

These charts are guidelines for not only squatting, pulling, and pressing, but variations of the Olympic lifts or the deadlift. It should teach proper planning order to control volume and intensity zones and suitable bar speed.

330-Max Percentage, 400-Max percentage and 450-Max Percentage

Percent	Weight (pounds)	Reps	Band Tension	Total Volume
50%	150	9x3 Reps	75 lb	4,050 lb
50%	150	9x3 Reps	75 lb	4,050 lb
50%	150	9x3 Reps	75 lb	4,050 lb
Percent	Weight (pounds)	Reps	Band Tension	Total Volume
50%	200	9x3 Reps	100 lb	5,400 lb
50%	200	9x3 Reps	100 lb	5,400 lb
50%	200	9x3 Reps	100 lb	5,400 lb
Percent	Weight (pounds)	Reps	Band Tension	Total Volume
50%	225	9x3 Reps	125 lb	6,000 lb
50%	225	9x3 Reps	125 lb	6,000 lb
50%	225	9x3 Reps	125 lb	6,000 lb

Periodization by Percentages

Westside constantly talks about the value of controlling loading by a percentage of a one rep max. This solves the problem of overtraining or detraining. I found the importance of this after applying the advice of A.S. Prilepin's chart for loading at different percentages in *Managing the Training of Weightlifters*. He listed how many repetitions per set as well as how many lifts per workout. His findings show that if the number of lifts is vastly under or over, the training effect decreases. The subject can be thoroughly studied in this book. A sound conclusion was discussed there by A.S. Medvedev in a section titled *"A System of Multi-Year Training in Weightlifting."*

At the 1964 Olympics, Leonid Zhabotinsky had won the gold medal. Zhabotinsky's volume remained the same for the next two years although his intensity decreased. The result of this was no increase in his total. In 1967, the training intensity was raised and once again the totals started to rise. How does a sportsman increase his lift without overtraining or detraining while maintaining correct bar speed? The answer: a three-week pendulum wave for speed strength development because it controls volume and intensity for one's strength level.

Below is an outline of a 50-pound jump to raise a squat from 400 pounds to 700 pounds. If strength and speed have not increased by a great deal, the athlete and coach have failed.

400-Pound Max Squat

Percent	Weight (pounds)	Reps	Lifts	Band Tension	Volume
50%	200	12x2	24	25%	4,800 lb
55%	220	12x2	24	25%	5,280 lb
60%	240	10x2	20	25%	4,800 lb
Bar Speed is 0.8 m/s avg.					

450-Pound Max Squat

Percent	Weight (pounds)	Reps	Lifts	Band Tension	Volume
50%	225	12x2	24	25%	5,400 lb
55%	250	12x2	24	25%	6,000 lb
60%	270	10x2	20	25%	5,400 lb
Bar Speed is 0.8 m/s avg.					

500-Pound Max Squat

Percent	Weight (pounds)	Reps	Lifts	Band Tension	Volume
50%	250	12x2	24	25%	6,000 lb
55%	275	12x2	24	25%	6,600 lb
60%	300	10x2	20	25%	6,000 lb
Bar Speed is 0.8 m/s avg.					

550-Pound Max Squat

Percent	Weight (pounds)	Reps	Lifts	Band Tension	Volume
50%	275	12x2	24	25%	6,600 lb
55%	300	12x2	24	25%	7,200 lb
60%	330	10x2	20	25%	6,600 lb
Bar Speed is 0.8 m/s avg.					

600-Pound Max Squat

Percent	Weight (pounds)	Reps	Lifts	Band Tension	Volume
50%	300	12x2	24	25%	7,200 lb
55%	330	12x2	24	25%	7,920 lb
60%	360	10x2	20	25%	7,200 lb
Bar Speed is 0.8 m/s avg.					

650-Pound Max Squat

Percent	Weight (pounds)	Reps	Lifts	Band Tension	Volume
50%	325	12x2	24	25%	7,800 lb
55%	355	12x2	24	25%	8,520 lb
60%	390	10x2	20	25%	7,800 lb
Bar Speed is 0.8 m/s avg.					

Look at the waves carefully. The bar speed remains the same during each wave regardless of the bar weight. Why is it important regardless if it is 400-pound max as a freshman or a 700-pound max as a senior? Accommodating resistance with bands or chains must be implemented to promote accelerating strength. If strength does not increase, speed won't increase either. To become stronger, volume must increase at the same intensity zones. Each max has a correct amount of volume. Just like the great Olympic champion L. Zhabotinsky found, if volume stays the same, the results will stagnate. This multi-year system perfects skills as strength is increased, and one should be able to use perfect form while using moderate weights. Remember the equation F=ma. Three days or 72 hours later, a max effort day must occur. This builds absolute strength.

Experts like A.P. Bondarchuk theorize that by perfecting skills, an individual utilizes strength gains. My idea is that to increase muscular strength you must perfect skills by increasing coordination. I am sure neither Bondarchuk nor I are totally correct, but this system blends both together. This system is simple mathematics.

Look at the raise in strength at 50-pound intervals (preceding charts). The volume climbs 600 pounds at the same intensities. Let's look at the bench press, although any style of pressing can use this system, such as overhead press, push jerk in front or behind head. The bench waves stay at one constant percent with barbell weight. The change in resistance is made by changing the amount of bands, chains or weight releasers.

Bench Press Chart

Percent	Weight (pounds)	Reps	Lifts	Band Tension	Volume
50%	350	12x2	24	25%	8,400 lb
55%	385	12x2	24	25%	9,240 lb
60%	420	10x2	20	25%	8,400 lb
Bar Speed is 0.8 m/s avg.					

Four Examples of a Three-Week Wave 300-pound Max Clean/Snatch

As can be seen in the four examples, it is the method of accommodating resistance so to develop maximal tension throughout the entire range of motion. Many times exercise machines use a special cam with variable lever arms as to apply a larger force at the weakest point of the strength curve (V.M. Zatsiorsky). This is done with varying totals of band tension, chain weight or using the lightened method with different amounts of unloading in the bottom. Real weight must be employed. Machines build muscle, not motion. Always use three different grips, none being outside the power lines.

300-pound Max Clean/Snatch Lightened Method

Percent	Weight (pounds)	Reps	Lifts	Total Volume
50%	150	9x3	27	85 lb
50%	150	9x3	27	85 lb
50%	150	9x3	27	85 lb
Percent	Weight (pounds)	Reps	Lifts	Total Volume
50%	150	9x3	27	80 lb
50%	150	9x3	27	80 lb
50%	150	9x3	27	80 lb
Percent	Weight (pounds)	Reps	Lifts	Chain Weight and Band Tension
50%	150	9x3	27	80 lb; 25 lb at top
50%	150	9x3	27	80 lb; 25 lb at top
50%	150	9x3	27	80 lb; 25 lb at top
Percent	Weight (pounds)	Reps	Lifts	Unload Weight
80%	240	9x3	27	60 lb
80%	240	9x3	27	60 lb
80%	240	9x3	27	60 lb

SPEED PULLS

Westside uses three types of speed pulls after speed squats:

1. SPEED PULLS ON FLOOR WITH BANDS

The math is roughly 30 percent band tension at lockout plus 50 percent bar weight of a one rep max. A 700-pound deadlifter would use a 345-pound bar weight plus 220 pounds at top of lift. A three-week wave would look like this:

700-POUND DEADLIFT

Wide Sumo on Floor				
Week	**Weight (pounds)**	**Reps**	**Sets**	**Band Tension**
1	345	3	10	220 lb
2	345	8	8	220 lb
3	345	6	6	220 lb
Conventional Rack Pulls with Bands				
Week	**Weight (pounds)**	**Reps**	**Sets**	**Band Tension**
4	345	2	10	250 lb
5	345	2	8	250 lb
6	345	2	6	250 lb
Close Sumo on Floor				
Week	**Weight (pounds)**	**Reps**	**Sets**	**Band Tension**
7	345	1	10	280 lb
8	345	1	8	280 lb
9	345	1	6	280 lb
Conventional Rack Pulls				
Week	**Weight (pounds)**	**Reps**	**Sets**	**Band Tension**
10	315	3	10	350 lb
11	315	3	8	350 lb
12	315	3	6	350 lb

2. ULTRA-WIDE SUMO DEADLIFTS WITH BAR WEIGHT 700-POUND DEADLIFT

Notice how a three-week wave is constantly altered to avoid accommodation. The weight may vary or the stance may change from sumo to conventional to ultra-wide sumo to rack pulls.

3. BOX DEADLIFTS

Considering box deadlifts, I suggest placing the bar on mats to raise the elevation of the barbell. This maintains the feel of the mechanics of the bar. The band tension also changes each cycle or on the fourth week. The loading graphs are based on a 700-pound max deadlift. All one needs is to reduce the amount of bar weight and band tension by 50 percent.

350-POUND DEADLIFT

Ultra-Wide Sumo with Barbell weight				
Week	Weight (pounds)	Reps	Sets	
12	500	3	10	
14	500	3	8	
15	500	3	6	
Wide Sumo on Floor 350-Pound Deadlift				
Week	Weight (pounds)	Reps	Sets	Band Tension
1	175	1	10	110 lb
2	175	1	8	110 lb
3	175	1	6	110 lb
Conventional Rack Pulls with Bands				
Week	Weight (pounds)	Reps	Sets	Band Tension
4	175	2	10	125 lb
5	175	2	8	125 lb
6	175	2	6	125 lb

Close Sumo on Floor				
Week	Weight (pounds)	Reps	Sets	Band Tension
7	175	1	10	140 lb
8	175	1	8	140 lb
9	175	1	6	140 lb

Again, note that each three-week wave is somehow different. It may be the bar weight, it can be band tension, or it could be altered by a different stance or how far the bar is off of the floor. By using a power rack or by placing plates on rubber mats, one can also stand on a two-inch or four-inch box. A 350-pound deadlift is half or 50 percent of the volume of a 700-pound deadlift. Mathematics is an essential part of weightlifting because a lifter must control the total volume of a training session. The intensity zones or what percent of a one rep max must also be considered. As graphs in this text show, the volume must be highest on speed strength day while the intensities are moderately low to moderate—50 percent to 80 percent. The max effort day would require the intensity zone to possibly be 100 percent plus, allowing the volume to be as low as 35 percent to 50 percent. The loading for power cleans and power snatches without bands or chains must also be regulated.

The training of top weightlifters must use a wide variety of exercises, not just power cleans and power snatches, but the classical clean, jerk and snatch. More than 50 percent of all training must be comprised of special exercises such as: back raises, belt squats, inverse curls, box jumps, Reverse Hypers®, Goodmornings, and a wide variety of pulls, squats, jerks and presses.

The Soviets were experts at calculating volume and intensities. Men like A.S. Prilepin, A.D. Ermakov and N.S. Atanasov provided studies in managing and training of weightlifters that determined how many snatch and clean jerks were to be done in a single workout and how many reps, sets, and at what percent these should be monitored. Although my observations are very close to theirs, I find it is important to train optimally, not maximally or minimally. Plus, we keep percents for weightlifting five percent lower than their recommendations. The data from 1975 by A.D. Ermakov and N.S. Atansov in *Managing and Training of Weightlifters* found roughly 50 percent of the lifts fell between 75 percent and 85 percent. While it is fully recognized this is where speed strength is developed, many lifters today did not grow up doing weightlifting. I propose performing five percent less on each three-week wave.

EXAMPLE:

300-Pound Power Clean				
Week	Percent	Reps	Sets	Lifts
1	70%	3	6	18
2	75%	3	6	18
3	80%	3	4	12

Conventional Rack Pull				
Week	Weight (pounds)	Reps	Sets	Band Tension
10	160	3	10	175 lb
11	160	3	8	175 lb
12	160	3	6	175 lb
Ultra Wide Sumo with Barbell weight				
Week	Weight (pounds)	Reps	Sets	
13	175	3	10	
14	175	3	8	
15	175	3	6	

This workout can be done after Friday's speed squat workout. You should rest between sets about 90 seconds. This requires good GPP. After all, you are an athlete, right?

250-Pound Power Snatch

This workout can follow a max effort workout on Monday. First, do a max exercise. Example: Low box squats, overhead squat, Goodmornings, box pulls, rack pulls, heavy sled pulls for 60 yards, then rest 90 seconds. After a heavy lift, a clean or snatch feels lighter and faster. Add variety like band tension of different amounts. I give credit to five great men: Ermakov, Atanasov and Prilephin's in *Managing and Training of Weightlifters*, and Verkhoshansky and Medvedev in *A System of Multi-Year Training in Weightlifting*, for not only guiding my career since 1983, but undoubtedly saving my lifting life. I have slightly modified the volume and intensity by using somewhat lighter lifts. One reason is due to a lesser background in GPP and physical preparedness, and second, we use a lot of powerlifting exercises.

A lifter must wave back down after a three-week wave, but also change something, at least slightly. Vary the amount of bar weight, band tension, chains, weight, box height, pin height, or bars to avoid accommodation. The speed day volume will be the highest while intensity will be at a low 40 percent to moderate 80 percent. Seventy-two hours later on max effort day requires intensity to be a max of that particular day, hopefully meaning a near all-time max or an all-time max on some special exercise. It is gaining strength in the right special exercises that brings forth a next personal best in a clean or snatch or jerk.

If an individual fully understands the process or percents, he will never over train or under train. He needs to alternate weak muscle groups that lead to injuries and constantly make progress until he reaches his sport's potential. Use three, three-week waves before trying a new max. In the beginning, progress is easy, but as an individual starts to lift weights that only a handful have ever lifted, it becomes more difficult. It's lonely at the top.

250-Pound Power Snatch

Week	Percent	Reps	Sets	Lifts
1	70%	3	6	18
2	75%	3	6	18
3	80%	3	4	12

For the weightlifter, it is most important to raise absolute strength to overcome larger loads; to become faster is secondary to strength. This is a common misconception of weightlifting coaches in the United States. After all, world record weights move slower than training weights. An athlete must use the optimal weight for his strength. The amount of work and rest must be monitored as well as movement tempo. Weightlifting requires a great deal of speed and strength. While speed is, of course, a major factor, speed is necessary to lift with strength-speed for the development of quick strength.

Weights are 100 percent plus of a max lift. This can be and should be done on max effort workout days. As strength and speed increase at each percent, an individual achieves a new max to work from. This yields a larger training volume. Consider the chart that shows how a 400-max squat volume was 4,800 pounds, and how a 500-max squat would require 6,000 pounds of volume. For every 50 pounds gained in a max squat, a rise in volume of 600 pounds will be factored in at the same 50 percent to 60 percent. There is much to consider when perfecting form: GPP, recovery methods, relaxation, and above all a selection of the correct special exercises for the individual. Mental, physical, and emotional maturity needs to be considered. Many require a plan. This is a plan for an individual's current strength level and how to raise it correctly. The amount of rest between sets must be a factor because this can be critical for recovery. The percent of a one rep max and the volume the training plan calls for is imperative. This is the interval method, much like track athletes use.

With small weights that football players use for speed development, the rest between sets of two reps represents the majority of football plays four to seven seconds. An individual should and must recover in 40 seconds for 12 sets of two reps. For explosive strength development, 24 sets of two reps can be performed with 40 second intervals, which builds explosive strength in a fatigue state and represents training at 70 percent to 85 percent. The rest must be 60 seconds to 90 seconds between sets. Max effort work can require two to four minutes rest between singles, which is dependent of the athlete's level of physical preparedness.

The findings of experts like A.S. Prilepin in *Managing and Training of Weightlifters* discovered too many reps per set can change a reduction in force development. It is best to perform high sets and low reps for recovery. The high rep sets should only include special exercises for individual muscles. While his recommendation was with weights at 70 percent to 90 percent, I have concluded that 40 percent to 60 percent provides the same results. If one watches a ball bounce with every preceding bounce, the rebound has less height. Why? It's due to the loss of kinetic energy.

The human body works in a similar fashion with the expenditure of kinetic energy in the soft tissue and muscle fatigue. Repetitions range for explosive strength or explosive power. Starting strength is inherited due to the amount or ratio of fast and slow twitch muscle fiber in the body. The same holds true for absolute strength where one lifts his maximum weight with no time limit. After years of following the guidelines set forth by A.S. Prilepin, A.D. Ermakov, N.S. Atanasov and many other sports experts from the former Soviet Union and along with my own experience over 50 years, I have suggestions for planning sets, reps per workout at a predetermined intensity zone for any athlete after a period of three years of general preparation.

If bar speed is reduced, the set must be stopped because of a power reduction. Pay close attention to the minimal and maximal total reps and amount of lifts per workout. For most, the optimal number of lifts is more beneficial.

Percent	Reps	Lifts
40%	4 to 8	36
50%	3 to 6	36
60%	3 to 6	30
70%	3 to 6	18
80%	2 to 4	15
90%	1 to 2	4 to 10
If you are greatly above or below the optimal number, the training affects are diminished. These are the recommendations of Lou Simmons, the author, that you do no fewer than 24 and no more than 48.		
50%: no less than 24 and no more than 48		
60%: no less than 20 and no more than 40		
70%: no less than 12 and no more than 24		
80%: no less than 10 and no more than 20		
90%: no less than 4 and no more than 10		

How To Change Volume at the Same Intensity Zone

Increase your three maxes for a front squat, safety squat bar, and of course, a regular squat bar max. Here is how:

500-POUND MAX FRONT SQUAT

Week	Percent	Weight (pounds)	Reps	Lifts	Volume
1	50%	250	12X2	24	6,000 lb
2	55%	275	12X2	24	6,600 lb
3	60%	300	10X2	20	6,000 lb
Bar Speed is 0.8 m/s avg.					

600-POUND MAX SAFETY SQUAT BAR

Week	Percent	Weight (pounds)	Reps	Lifts	Volume
1	50%	300	12X2	24	7,200 lb
2	55%	330	12X2	24	7,920 lb
3	60%	360	10X2	20	7,200 lb
Bar Speed is 0.8 m/s avg.					

700-POUND MAX REGULAR SQUAT BAR

Week	Percent	Weight (pounds)	Reps	Lifts	Volume
1	50%	350	12X2	24	8,400 lb
2	55%	385	12X2	24	9,240 lb
3	60%	420	10X2	20	8,400 lb
Bar Speed is 0.8 m/s avg.					

You must pay close attention to these graphs for continued progress in classical barbell lifts including the following: Olympic weightlifting lifts, powerlifting lifts, special squats, Goodmornings, pulls and pressing exercises. Combining mathematics, physics, and biomechanics, your true potential can be reached.

Figure 3: As you can see by this chart, the ratio between barbell and classical lifts is 20 percent barbell exercises and 80 percent special exercises. This is proven by the research done at Westside Barbell by Joe Lasko on powerlifts and Olympic weightlifting as well as track and field. Because athletes are built biomechanically different, it can be dangerous to perform high repetition barbell lifts, as the weakest component of the human can become fatigued and sustain injuries. It is much safer to do special exercises directed to a particular muscle group that may be lacking.

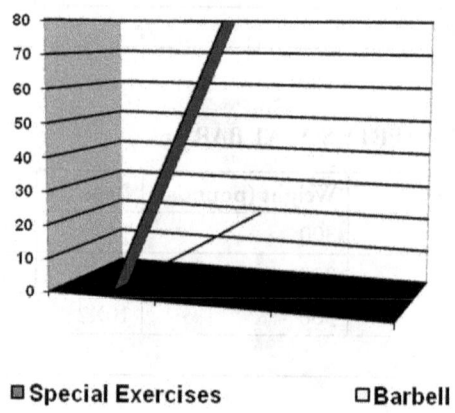

Circa Max Performed to a Parallel Box.

Max Weight	Bar Weight	Weight Percent	Band Tension	Band Tension
800 lb	500 lb	62%	375 lb	47%
850 lb	550 lb	61%	375 lb	44%
900 lb	600 lb	66%	375 lb	42%
950 lb	650 lb	68%	375 lb	39%
1000 lb	600 lb	60%	440 lb	44%
1050 lb	650 lb	62%	440 lb	42%
1100 lb	700 lb	64%	440 lb	40%
1150 lb	750 lb	65%	440 lb	38%

DELAYED TRANSFORMATION CONNECTING CIRCA-MAX PHASE

The data derived in this section is from Ivan Abadzhiev, V.Y. Verkhoshansky and A.S. Medvedev.

The results at the contest, of course, are of most importance. It requires two proven methods of periodization.

Delayed transformation is a period of reducing the amount of volume and reducing the intensity zone somewhat to induce the highest level of sporting skill at contest time.

It was brought about through track and field and Olympic weightlifting from the former Soviet Union. For the squat training, it starts at 35 days out from contest date. Roughly 50 percent sets are done for the optimal amount of sets and lifts. The same is true for 28 days out of your contest.

Now, it is interrupted at 21 days, but for Westside, it is a new or all-time record on a box squat. See the circa-max chart above (circa-max means near max). A circa-max phase is performed with weights in the range of 90 percent to 97 percent if a one rep max. Lifts at those percentages are four minimal, seven optimal and 10 maximal. Westside uses the optimal method, utilizing seven lifts on the circa max day.

An 800-pound squatter after a warm up performs the following:

- 330-pound bar weight x two reps + 375 pounds band tension
- 370-pound bar weight x two reps + 375 pounds band tension
- 420-pound bar weight x one rep + 375 pounds band tension
- 470-pound bar weight x one rep + 375 pounds band tension
- P.R. 510-pound bar weight x one rep + 375 pounds band tension If an athlete can perform this weight, and if the box height is correct (parallel and good form), he will break a new squat record. During the second week of circa-max, the lifter will work up to approximately 370 pounds for a single. This concludes the circa-max phase. It represents 21 days out and 14 days out.

Now more recovery time is needed. Seven days out large athletes (275 pounds and up) will not squat, but do only special exercises. Two hundred and forty-two pound athletes and lighter can squat light. For example, 330 pounds x 2 x 2 with no band tension, or if you like, 140 pounds of band tension.

As you see, Westside divides the delayed transformation phase in two parts: with extreme stimulus at 21 days out, then back to the delayed transformation through 14 days out to assure all three lifts are at their max on contest day.

This chart is the combined efforts of 75 men who have officially squatted from 800 pounds up to 1,205 pounds. Look carefully at the bar weight percentage and the band tension percentage.

As a lifter progresses from 800 pounds to 950 pounds, the bar percentage goes from 62 percent to 68 percent, causing the band tension to go from 47 percent to 39 percent. This means the bar percent goes up six percent while the band tension goes down eight percent. Let it be noted as well that at 1,000 pounds to 1,150 pounds, the bar percent goes up five percent while the band tension goes down six percent.

I am asked about scientific studies and I can tell you that no one besides Westside has such a study with world class strength athletes. Ours is a work of more than twenty years of experiments. More can be learned about the Delayed Transformation Phase on pg. 30 in *Science and Practice of Strength Training* (Zatsiorsky Circa Max Method 1995; Verkhoshansky 2009 *Supertraining*).

WORKOUTS

1. Clean pull, followed by squat clean

2. Jerk barbell taken from stands

3. Clean and jerk starting with barbell below knees

4. Push jerk followed by jerk, barbell taken from stands

5. Clean pull with four stops upwards

6. Power clean, squat, then jerk

7. Clean and jerk starting with barbell at knee level

8. Clean pull from the floor

9. Jerk from behind the head

10. Clean and jerk starting with barbell below the knees

11. Push jerk with barbell taken from stands

12. Clean pull with a medium hand spacing

13. Squat followed by jerk behind the head

14. Classic clean and jerk from the floor

15. Power clean starting with barbell at knee level

16. Clean pull standing on a block

17. Push jerk from behind the head followed by overhead squat

18. Front squat followed by jerk

19. Clean pull starting with the barbell at knee level

20. Power clean from the floor

21. Half jerk followed by the jerk with barbell taken from stands

22. Clean pull slowly up plus lower slowly

23. Push jerk after power clean

24. Power clean, push jerk, then overhead squat

25. Clean pull to knee level

Special Notes

PROGRESS IS BASED ON PERIODIZATION

A weightlifter has to build a strong back and legs to reach the top. I read that David Rigert could squat 10 reps with 675 pounds at 198-pound body weight. I also read a story about David bombing out of a major meet with a 352-pound snatch. David took some time off afterwards. When he returned to a lifting hall, a lifter was snatching the same 352 pounds that he bombed out with. David's friend noticed he was glaring at the bar and realized what David was thinking. He said "Don't do it!" David (in street clothes) approached the bar loaded with 352 pounds and proceeded to snatch it with no warm-up. These two stories tell the author just how strong David's legs and back were. This could account for David breaking world records.

I have had several novice weightlifters visit Westside to train. By the author's system of combinations of method training, they will break their record in the clean or snatch nine out of 10 times in just 30 minutes. Many times they have been stuck for months without a PR. After setting a new clean or snatch record, which is low by any standards due to low back strength, they are unable to recover from the clean (due to even lower leg strength). You must raise max strength to reach the top. Many think that speed is most important due to the fact that you can only make the lift with the amount of weight you do in the weakest portion of the lift. It does no good to clean 400 pounds if your front squat is 360 pounds; or to snatch 300 pounds if your overhead squat is 280 pounds. The legs must have an over abundance of strength compared to your clean or snatch. I constantly hear that the squat only has to be a small percent of your clean and jerk. This is completely WRONG! Not only do you have to recover from the clean, but you also must have a reserve of leg strength for the thrust in the jerk.

Weightlifters in the former Soviet Union had a wide base before weight training began. This wide base lead to, at least, basic leg strength. A good coach or lifter should know that the top five interdependent correlations for maximal results are:

1. Power Clean
2. Power Snatch

3. Clean

4. Overhead Squat

5. Clean from the Hang

This is according to *Managing the Training of Weightlifters*.

The author's findings have concluded that when the squat was raised, the pulls increased as well. So what is the answer? It has been said that some lifters squat six times a week, but with no great results. The author has viewed several squat workouts and found they are too slow to produce proper force. The percentages should range between 75 percent and 85 percent with only barbell weight, or 50 percent to 60 percent with 25 percent band tension at the top for three-week pendulum waves. The bar should move at .8 to .9 m/s—this is force equals mass times acceleration. I hope this sounds familiar as it is Newton's Second Law: $F=MA$. Why is this so important? Let's look at the definition of work:

In physics, work is defined as the product of net force and the displacement throughout where that force is exerted or $W=Force$. If work is a barbell lift, clean, or squat, then how can one move the same or larger weight faster? The answer: by becoming more powerful. In physics, power is divided by the time used to do the work or $P=wt$. This simply means the more powerful lifter can do the work in less time. Now we are finally getting to the point. Yes, we need a stronger squat! But, squatting repeatedly is not the answer. The problem is the Law of Accommodation. If one does the same exercise with the same training load repeatedly, the performance will decrease over time. Many would think this is the definition of insanity, but science refers to it as accommodation, a biological law.

The pulls are the same. They, too, will stop increasing poundage if done repeatedly. The Westside conjugate system calls for breaking down the squats and pulls into segments. You must increase leg strength—meaning calves, hamstrings, and quads—into special exercises for each muscle group.

SPECIAL EXERCISES:

- Leg Presses
- Step Ups
- Glute/Ham Raises
- Inverse Curls
- Calf Raises
- Sled Pulls
- Wheel Barrows
- Back Raises
- Goodmornings
- Reverse Hypers
- Belt Squats
- Box Jumping
- Upright Rows
- Bent Over Rows
- Pull-ups

These are some small special exercises that can make an incredible difference in building a strong squat and pull. Why does Westside want you to use a wide stance for squatting? Because you have never worked those muscles! Those unused muscles are contributing to lifting more weight. Wide-stance straight-leg style deadlifts and wide-stance arched-back power cleans, for example.

Side Note: I was having a discussion about the deadlift for Olympic lifters when a well-known author said that a powerlifting deadlift would not work for an Olympic lifter due to the round backed style. I replied "What about the sumo style where the back is arched?" He had no clue. This is the problem with most (not all) Olympic coaches—they do not have a clue about anything that can improve strength. Perfect form must be taught in the early stages then a constant increase in strength must come to win bigger and bigger contests. I hope this makes sense to you. Hardly anyone has a perfect body for any sport, especially weightlifting. Everyone has some muscle groups stronger than others. Some have very strong backs and not so strong legs. Of course, the back will do the majority of the work load. But what if that individual builds his or her legs up to match their back strength? They could, of course, lift heavier weights and be much safer, too, because the work would be distributed throughout the body.

I have asked Tom Eiseman (780 at 181 pounds) where he felt the deadlift the most and his reply was very profound. His answer was "everywhere." Only small special exercises can bring up lacking or weak muscle groups. An example is ab work. If one did no direct ab work, abs would be weak leading to back ailments. If you are very strong, but slow, you must work on your explosive and speed strength. But don't neglect your strength speed—the one thing you are blessed with. Train what you don't have. But, remember, it does no good to be strong in the wrong exercises.

If Medvedev had more than 75 barbell exercises for the weightlifter, there were, of course, many more small special exercises. For a single muscle group, many were on special machines; then there are Kettlebells, alternating close grips for snatches and wide grips for cleans, to name just a few examples.

Last, but not least, please read! I have a large list of books for anyone who will read them. I used this material to build the strongest powerlifting gym in the history of powerlifting. As of July 2014, Westside had five of the top 10 totals of all-time. This includes the highest total of 3,005 at 271 and the top two coefficient totals of all-time. Plus, the number one women's coefficient totals of all-time. Also, the top coefficient squats for men and women and the top coefficient bench press for men and women in a power meet. This Westside Method is 33 years in the making. Its methods are from weightlifting and track and field. The author re-engineered the Soviet System to fit not only powerlifting, but all sports.

Warning: there is no such thing as five rep systems, three rep systems, or the single rep system, nor the Cube Method, 5-3-1 Method or the Nebraska System. These systems are fantasy.

There are four systems that are proven by science: The Maximal Effort Method, the Dynamic Effort Method, the Submaximal Effort Method, and the Repeated Effort Method. Westside thanks the great former Soviet Union sports scientists such as V.M Zatsiorsky, as well as Dr. Mel Siff of *Supertraining* fame (A good friend; may he rest in peace.). Along with Y.V Verkhoshansky, Mel was a true genius in the development of sports science. And don't forget Dr. Isaac Newton the father of the laws of motion. Without these great men and a long list of others that are mentioned in the references, we wouldn't be where we are today.

CHAPTER 4

FUNDAMENTALS OF JUMPING

Kneeling Jumps

One must change the total volume of training by introducing an activity, such as jumping, in exchange for a portion of weight lifting. Jumping combines strength, speed, and, of course, coordination, therefore it is an inseparable part of sports training during general sport-specific preparation. Looking at the total volume of training, special means must be rotated at all times to avoid accommodation. When introducing a high volume of jumping, some pulls and squats must be reduced. Always think optimal. If your muscles are sore from weight training, your jumps will suffer, and vice versa. A pendulum with all styles of periodization must be integrated.

Here is the simple method to build a solid foundation for your jumping program:

To prepare the athlete for jumping, start out sitting on the floor with feet out in front and press a barbell or Kettlebell overhead. This will build the entire body for the rigors of jumping, as well as landing.

Next, sit on knees and then jump onto feet. When possible, add weight to the back. Note: a Westside record is 310 pounds. Next, power clean from the kneeling position. After mastering the kneeling power clean, jump onto feet while power cleaning. Follow this with a snatch while kneeling. Then proceed to jump onto feet while snatching. Next, split snatch while kneeling. Another good exercise is simply jumping vertically as high as possible. These can be done freely or onto a box or platform for height. Again, be sure to add weight when possible for all exercises.

Remember, you must build a high level of strength to begin jumping. As explosive strength grows from jumping, it is most important to raise your absolute strength through resistance training. Without a plan, you plan to fail.

This system of jumping and weight training should be implemented with a three-week pendulum wave, for easy monitoring, where speed, strength, and correct muscle training occur together.

You will learn that strength training will increase coordination while increasing strength in a locking muscle group. This also acts as a preventative measure to limiting injuries.

COMBINATIONS OF RESISTANCE JUMPING METHODS

As Verkhoshansky warns, depth jumps can be very dangerous. But Westside is known for the development of absolute strength and for rigorous attention to plans and safety. Westside has a high school girl jump onto a 50½-inch box. Westside also had an intern jump onto a 63½-inch box after just two months, starting at a meager 44-inch box. How? The answer is by jumping with weight and a combination of weight plus band resistance. As we know, it is not the fall that kills you, but rather the landing—no joke. Remember, you are falling at $9.8^m/_s$ when landing.

Of course, at the start of the free fall, the velocity is zero. But, because the body or its mass and velocity causes momentum or $F = ma$, this makes the landing greatly dangerous. But, by jumping upward with a powerful effort upon landing, velocity is near zero as one lands on the box while gravity assists the falling downward. The box jumping most overcomes the force of gravity plus the athlete's weight plus added resistance. After all, one must have great strength to jump high. In order to jump higher, you must first become stronger. It is that simple.

If the ground reaction forces are known as a function of time $F(T)$ during the jump and the jumper's mass (m) is known, the velocity as a function of time $V(T)$, and the power as a function of time $P(T)$, can be calculated.

JUMPING METHODS

BOX SQUAT JUMPING

Perform a box squat onto a 12-inch box by sitting completely down and rocking backwards while swinging arms back and lifting feet off of the ground. Next, swing arms forward while slamming feet into the floor and jump up onto a second box of a predetermined height. By sitting down on the box, the athlete breaks up the eccentric-concentric chain. Sitting on a box is defined as a collision. The law of conservation of momentum also allows us to analyze collisions between the box and the athlete. It is not a perfect collision, like a pool ball hitting a second ball; they would be equal. As the athlete sits on the box, part of his kinetic energy is transferred onto the box. Although the athlete is sitting on the box motionless, some of the muscles are stretching and then contracting, causing both a static contraction overcome by a dynamic effort, and at the same time some muscles are relaxed over by a dynamic effort. Both are thought to be the greatest combined methods for building explosive and absolute strength.

METHODS OF RESISTANCE

Ankle weights	Weight vest	Barbell + ankle weights
Kettlebell	Barbell	Kettlebell + ankle weights
Dumbbell	Bulgarian bag	Bulgarian bag + ankle weights
		Bulgarian bag + Kettlebell

This is a list of ten methods of resistance. There are more. Constantly rotate resistance each week. Keep records of weight, box height, and the combination of resistance used each week. Do 40 to 60 jumps per workout, twice weekly, separated by 72 hours.

It takes a high effort to jump up onto a box with body weight plus added weight. But, you will land at a near zero velocity, which is much safer. Box jumping is far superior to a vertical jump effort due to overcoming inhibitions, meaning fear of failure.

Many will hesitate before reacting, slowing the reaction time. Weightlifters are able to jump on boxes of great height due to their high level of strength. The author does not dispute the great effects of depth jumps, but many precautions must be taken. No such precautions are needed with resistance jumping.

When long jumping for distance, jump into a soft landing pit. If one holds Kettlebells or dumbbells when long jumping, release hand weights before impact.

Use a three-week pendulum wave for box jumping, meaning adding weight resistance each week in one method of resistance or in a combination of resistance. For example:

- 8 kg. Kettlebell in week 1
- 12 kg. Kettlebell in week 2
- 16 kg. Kettlebell in week 3

One could also raise the box height each week by two inches or four inches as a way to increase efforts of the athlete. On week four, go back down in resistance or box height and again increase work for week two and week three. Then, rollback again. This is a pendulum wave.

Box jumping can be done by sitting on a box, followed by a jump onto a second box. This is a proven concept of the development of both explosive strength, as well as absolute strength. This has been Westside's mainstay for 50 years now. While sitting on a box and relaxing the hip muscles, strongly flex the hips and glutes to overcome the relaxed phase concentrically. By doing a box squat correctly, it divides the eccentric-concentric phase where a portion of this action is isometric as well as a portion a relaxed phase. To box squat correctly, push glutes forward while pushing the knees apart as much as possible to activate the strong hip muscles. As one sits on the box, keep the back and abdominal muscles in an isometric contraction. Then, release the obliques and reflex them as powerfully as possible and jump off the box vertically or horizontally, depending on the jumping task. When sitting on the box, swing arms behind body, then during the raising or concentric phase, jump onto box of a predetermined height, or jump over an object for long jumping. Following this method has produced a 50½-inch box jump by a high school girl, and a 63½-inch box jump by an intern. As weight resistance is rotated, rotate box to box jumping to a modified dive style, meaning, dropping down much like a basketball player does while doing a center jump. While jumping, always remember the true definition of explosive power is to rapidly increase force (Tidow, 1990). The steeper the increase of strength in time, the greater the explosive strength. Much more detail can be found in *Explosive Power and Jumping Ability for All Sports*.

DEPTH JUMPS

They say there is a fine line between genius and insanity.

Depth jumps can be the same as they can either build a career or end a career. You must be an experienced coach before implementing depth jumps into your athletes programming.

Depth jumps are a very important part of raising explosive strength as well as reactive ability. Start with a low box, 12 to16 inches, and work up over time. For a highly advanced athlete, 36 to 39 inch depth jumps are optimal. When using a box above 42 inches, due to a much slower amortization phase, the strength developed is absolute strength, which is much like using a larger load with squatting or benching—the larger the load, the slower the reversal phase.

DEPTH JUMP CORRECTLY

Depth jumps are not only overused, but also done incorrectly. While they appear to be a simple undertaking, the action and implementation are actually very complex.

Drop Phase Execution

First one must use a box, or some other surface, to drop from. The drop phase, along with all proceeding phases, is very important. To begin, take a step forward with one leg. Do not bend your legs to jump forward but instead allow your body to drop forward. At the beginning of the fall, bring both feet together. The fall must be perpendicular to the ground.

Upon landing on the balls of both feet, quickly lean back onto the heels. Land as flexible as possible to cushion the fall, move both arms behind the body, then rebound. The landing phase must quickly transition to the take-off phase. Next, bring arms forward as powerfully as possible to achieve a flight phase. Now jump, or rebound, as high as possible while reaching to touch an object at a predetermined height. Try new records each time on several different boxes. Note all jumps should be measured by height, distance, or weight.

Note to coaches: depth jumps can have a very strong effect on the central nervous system, as well as the muscular, and skeletal systems. They can be dangerous, causing bones to break or tendons to snap. Thirty-six-inch boxes are optimal for only the highest skilled athletes who can squat at least two times their body weight. Large depths are not for high school or young college athletes. Do not drop jump when tired, or perform any other kind of jumps. Coaches, do not allow athletes with muscle pains to perform depth jumps. This is a major coaching malpractice. Verkhoshansky's insights on the shock training were profound in convincing the sports world in the volume of rebounding exercises. He was fascinated by the effects of the landing then rebounding of triple jumper around 1957. This work brought about by his experiments made Special Strength Training (SST) a main element of sports training.

HOW DO DEPTH JUMPS WORK?

Basic physics.

We know that a falling body accelerates at 9.8 m/s^2 near earth. The falling body has gravitational potential energy. Because of motion, kinetic energy is developed due to the athlete's mass and speed during the fall. This simply means that upon landing, the athlete has both potential and kinetic energy. Kinetic energy is the key value upon landing. Velocity is more important than mass or weight. This is why the effect of depth jumps is greater as the drop distance or timing space is increased. It is much more dangerous for a 300-pound lineman to drop off of a 36-inch box than a 150-pound dancer. Remember, to increase kinetic energy, it is better to increase velocity than mass. If one could triple velocity, it would increase kinetic energy nine times.

The amount of depth jumps should not exceed four sets of ten. In order to gain the most results for the less skilled athlete with a smaller GPP base, depth jumps should be limited to three sets of eight.

Much of this information came from *Special Strength Training: Manual for Coaches* by Y. Verkhoshansky and N. Verkhoshansky. Although Yuri may have passed away, his knowledge will last forever as guidelines for the author's special strength development plan. Other sports scientists that influenced the author are Henryk Sozanski, PhD, and, of course, Andrzej Lasocki.

JUMPING INSTRUCTIONS

Always choose an optimal box height to use depending on the level of preparedness of the athlete. While doing a 40-jump workout, it should be moderately difficult. Yet it should be possible, even on your worst training days. One must be able to do 40-jump workouts at the very end of a high volume barbell or sprinting workout. This means your GPP must be high. When doing such a high-volume workout, following it with jumping may not always be advisable, but again, it must be possible. This would prove the jumps were optimal. While experts on the subject, like T. Starzynski and H. Sozanski PhD, call for more jumps in a weekly, yearly, and multi-year program, they rely heavily on the volume of jumping to make it possible to increase the ability to jump, which then leads to more explosive power.

Yuri Verkhoshansky, from Russia, a country that leads the world in weightlifting, would limit the jumps, specifically depth jumps, to 30 to 40 per workout. His logic was to build a super strong body through many different forms of training linked together, which is the idea behind the Conjugate System. This called for 90 percent weights of two to three reps for two to three sets, then some method of jumping, meaning jumping up onto a box or depth jumps. Also, it would include jumping with 30 percent of a one rep max (RM) with jump squats. Verkhoshansky came to the conclusion that building absolute strength through weight training would contribute to building explosive strength for jumping ability.

While Verkhoshansky was influenced by weightlifting, your author was greatly influenced by powerlifting, a very similar method, but not by using very large weights that move slowly. Instead, by using the dynamic method in a weekly plan. The ratio of weights for ME workouts are three per week. Westside has more than a 90 percent rate for breaking an all-time record in a special barbell exercise. Seventy-two hours later, a dynamic method workout is performed with 30 to 40 percent of a one RM for explosive strength. This is done in a three-week wave period, or three-week wave using bar weight with band tension adding up to 75 to 85 percent at lockout. This system was made popular by the author and refers to the combinations of resistance methods found in *Supertraining*, by Dr. Mel Siff. For lower body development, perform an average of 80 lifts for speed strength per month. This calculates to 20 each week. Or, in a yearly plan, it is 960 lifts for acceleration and 156 for ME training. This practice can be followed throughout the entire year.

The Westside Conjugate Systems calls for maintaining all forms of strength at the same time, while it is still accepted to use a model of periodization, known as accumulation, intensification, and finally, transformation. There is still the old block training method, but this method does not work. It is where Block A would use maximal strength and special hypertrophy work. Then, Block B where the main objective is on increasing power to build maximal explosive force efforts in sports movements during competition. And, then finally, block C where technical work is mastered to make use of the training effects of the first two blocks. Let me repeat, however, this method does not work. The truth is, when you abandoned the previous block, you lead yourself to detraining, not training. This is why when Westside trains and then releases an athlete, such as a ballplayer, or a sprinter, they slow down instead of increasing their results. This occurs repeatedly with major colleges. And there is no excuse for this, as there can only be three reasons for it:

arrogance, ignorance, or a lack of knowledge—none of which are acceptable. While the greats of the past made it possible for many to achieve greatness, there must be constant improvement in programming, periodization, and restoration. All three velocities of strength must be trained simultaneously, while at the same time adding more of what the athlete needs, and reducing some volume of what they don't need as much. This is how to balance training. Technical skills must be learned early, in youth training, and maintained. Also, there should be no off season for a sprinter, nor any other sport activity. You must become better all year long, which can be accomplished using this system.

With Westside building a strong base, all methods can be increased all year long, without losing endurance. Include maximal speed and explosive strength, and training to increase them. Just use the delayed transformation phase. This means reducing the work 21 days out, then, tapering up to the important events. Midway through this discussion on jumping, I brought up the point that one must use a more efficient method for a yearly training program. If you drop strength and power training, your times will surely suffer. If you drop jumping exercises, your reaction times will deteriorate. None of this is advisable for faster running. What the author is asking the coach or athlete to do is different than physical maturity. As young boys and girls grow into teenagers, and eventually adults, they simply can do more work of any kind, as well as learn new sports tasks.

SPECIAL JUMPS

1	Knees to feet Bar on back 40 jumps	16	Jump onto optimal box with ankle weights 40 jumps
2	Knees to feet Power clean 40 jumps	17	Jump onto optimal box with weight vest 40 jumps
3	Knees to feet Power snatch 40 jumps	18	Jump onto optimal box with Bulgarian bag 40 jumps
4	Knees to feet Split snatch 40 jumps	19	Jump onto optimal box with Kettlebell and ankle weights 40 jumps
5	General jumping ability even boxes 40 jumps	20	Jump onto optimal box with Kettlebell and weight vest 40 jumps
6	Jump off high box onto low box Eccentric actions 40 jumps	21	Jump onto optimal box with Kettlebell and Bulgarian bag 40 jumps
7	Jump from low box to high box Concentric action 40 jumps	22	Jump onto optimal box with ankle weight and weight vest 40 jumps
8	General jumping ability Single leg 40 jumps	23	Jump onto optimal box with medicine ball 40 jumps
10	Low box to high box Concentric action, single leg 40 jumps	24	Static overcome by dynamic device 40 jumps
11	Barbell squat 90x2 reps, x2 sets Vertical jump 30-50%, 3x6 jumps	25	Jump using belt squat machine 40 jumps
12	Barbell squat 90% of 1RM, 2x2 reps	26	Jump using belt squat machine and ankle weights 40 jumps
13	Barbell squat 90% of 1RM, 2x2 reps Depth jumps 18-36" optimal box 40 jumps	27	Jump using belt squat machine and weight vest 40 jumps
14	Vertical jumps 60-70% of 1RM, 2x8 reps 2x8 low box to vertical jumps	28	Jump holding barbell in belt squat machine 40 jumps
15	Jump onto optimal box with Kettlebell 40 jumps	29	Sit on box and jump using belt squat machine 40 jumps

CHAPTER 5

WEIGHTED SLED PROGRAMING

ACCELERATION WORKOUTS

When doing sled work, reduce running by 30 percent. Westside uses a similar approach to acceleration, using an alternative weight on a sled. For women, use 10 kilograms or 25 pounds. For men, 20 kilograms or 45 pounds. For developing, the ability to move your legs faster than your competitor is a must, as well as increasing your stride while being able to maintain your top speed longer than everyone else and producing great ground force in minimal amount of time. But, how do you do this? The answer is pulling a weighted sled. For short running of up to 100 meters, sprint with a light-weight sled for 10 meters, 20 meters, 40 meters, and 60 meters. Up to this distance most gain speed. Use 10 kilograms for women, and 20 kilograms for men. Try to duplicate the start or do flying starts, but at all costs try to increase top speed and maintain it for as long as possible. This is for speed endurance. You must learn to relax while producing high force production.

WOROUTS FOR MAINTAINING TOP SPEED

Through much experience and experimentation, the correct weight on a sled should be equal to your bodyweight for up to 200 meter times, which means one should pull a sled. This method builds the ability to maintain top speed for as long as possible. Powerwalk as powerfully as possible for a set time. Example: 50 seconds. Set marker at the 20-second mark. Maintain the same style and weight, and try to cover more meters in the allotted 20 seconds. This forces the runner to push as hard and long as his or her ability will allow. This method will prolong the exertion phase.

For long distances, 400 meters to 800 meters, women should use 20 kilograms and men should use 90 kilograms. Pull a sled for a time slightly longer than your current best times. For example, 60 seconds for 400 meters and two minutes and 20 seconds for 800 meters.

For greater distance up to a marathon, women pull 10 kilograms and men pull 20 kilograms for as long as it takes to finish your race time.

POWER WALKING STYLE

Hook the sled to a belt around the waist. Begin walking with an over-stride style, landing on your heels. Do not lift knees high, but stay close to the ground. Duplicate body lean and arm swing as if you were running. But, it is not running, but rather power walking. This means that the sled should clank on each ground contact. It will feel, if done correctly, like a partial G.H.R Its purpose is to build the running muscles without back compression.

Sled Drag Forward & Backward

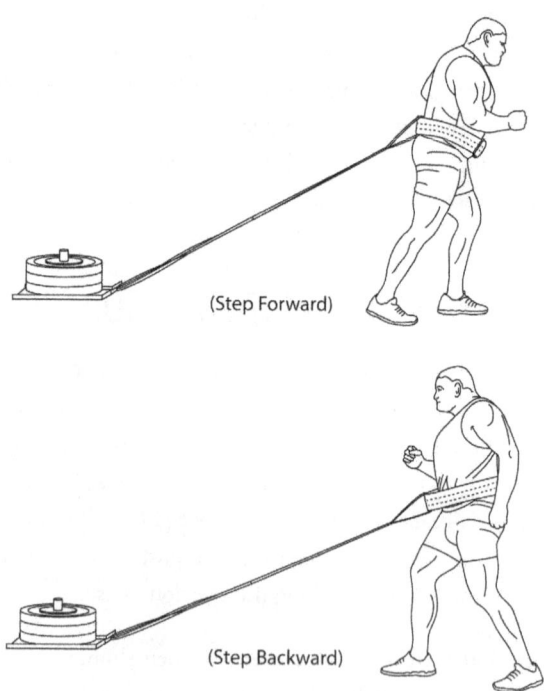

Fig. Power-walking with sled forward and backward. Low weight for long distance or heavy weight for short distance can be used.

ADDED RESISTANCE

Ankle weights can be added as well as a weight vest or Bulgarian bags. A weight suit can be used as well.

Power sled walking will improve your running performance by making running feel light after eliminating the sled. By building extra strength and power your stride frequency will improve greatly. It can improve running technique for all distances by improving muscle imbalances. It also will improve conditioning for running of all types. One can pull a sled uphill or downhill on all types of surfaces. By pulling a heavy sled with full muscular force, one can overcome the fear of injury while running at full speed. Pulling a sled can be used to correct leg, trunk and even arm movement errors due to the slow motion action that can be applied with a weighted sled. It is the Tai Chi of weight resistance.

Sidesteps (sample one)

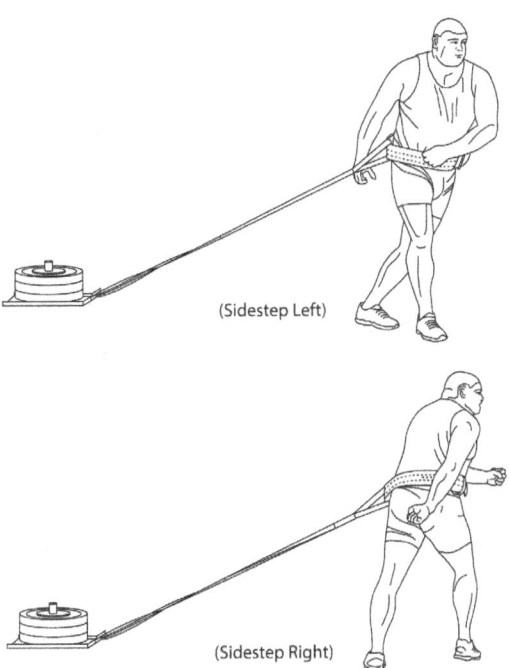

Fig. Sled dragging with sidesteps initiating with the forward leg

Sidesteps (sample two)

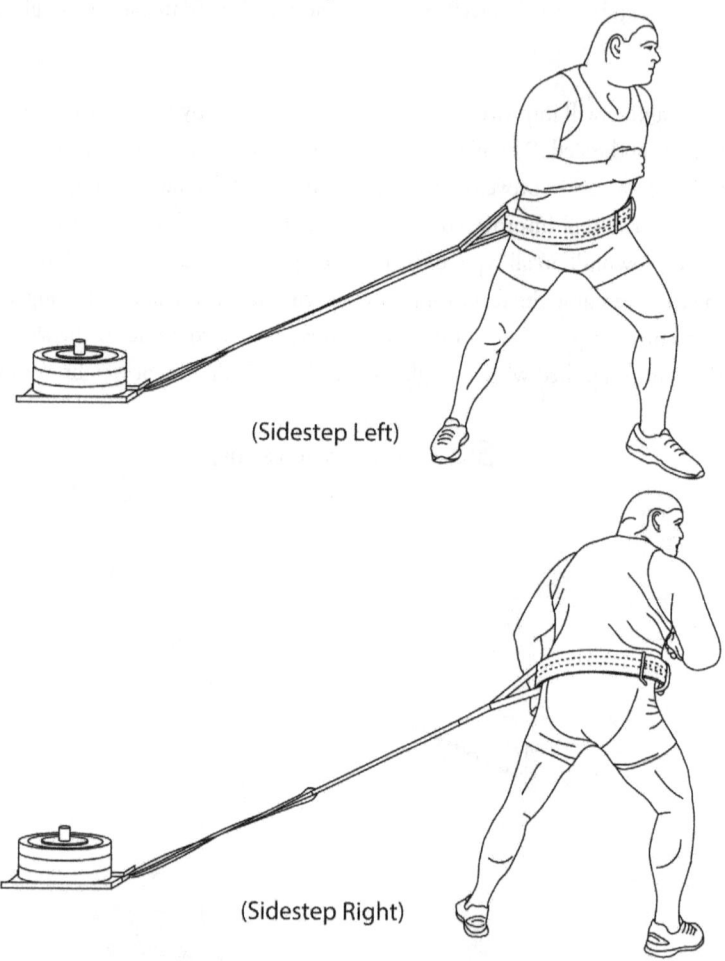

(Sidestep Left)

(Sidestep Right)

Fig. Sled dragging with sidesteps initiating with the back leg

CHAPTER 6
ENDURANCE

Endurance is the ability to counter fatigue. There is more to endurance than one may think. There are many types of fatigue. Mental fatigue can be a result of high competition with someone else or with oneself. Physical fatigue can be due to fear of injury. Emotional fatigue can be due to high level competitions or placing great emotional stress on oneself during training. This must be saved for a contest. Fatigue due to fear can be fear of an injury, or fear of failure. One such fear is not being able to make a new record on a box jump, according to Kukushkin, 1983. More information can be found in *The Science of Sports Training*, by Thomas Kurz.

To excel one must have a high pain tolerance and great motivation. For aerobic fitness, it is the amount of oxygen one can use in 60 seconds. After eight to 18 months maximal oxygen uptake will increase with dense training. It will level out even with more training. This means muscular endurance training is very important for the highest level runners.

Endurance is developed fairly fast compared to high levels of strength. First, to train for high endurance, one must learn to tolerate great fatigue. By combating fatigue, endurance increases through continuous training. It is important to stop endurance when form breaks down. Rest intervals should be altered to some extent, meaning going from one mile to three miles, and back to two miles. This will not allow the body to adapt fully. To adapt is never to adapt if a higher level of endurance is to be achieved. When running long races, heavy weight will not build endurance due to not being able to do high reps with 90 percent weight. But, raising maximal strength is a must for strength endurance. Frank Shorter was known for squatting 100 pounds for 100 reps. If Frank could do a one rep max with 200 pounds then 100 pounds would be 50 percent of his one rep max. If Frank could squat 300 pounds for a one rep max, 100 pounds would be $33^{1}/_{2}$ percent of his one rep max. This would be a more manageable weight for 100 reps. This bears out the fact that training at much different intensities can increase endurance. The strongest men and women need great endurance as well as the greatest need to raise absolute strength to some extent.

The author was a top ten powerlifter for 30 years. While doing an experiment with ten top-ranked powerlifters, I made 35 reps with 375 pounds. At the conclusion of the last rep, my oxygen and lactate threshold gave out simultaneously. This means the intensity was critical. By watching the end of a marathon, many times one has the oxygen to finish the race, but their legs lack muscular endurance; while others will not have a high enough oxygen consumption to finish the race. At other times, even a sprinter wins the marathon. So, there are many different things to consider. One must train with intensity equal to the event. While walking may have little effect on endurance, walking with resistance has great influence on endurance.

Example 1:

While training a D1 lineman to add endurance, he would walk three or four one-half mile walks with a 75-pound weight vest and 10- or 20-pound ankle weights plus carry 10-pound Kettlebells. After two months of Westside training with fast and slow weights, 80 resisted jumps per week, and no running other than lineman drills, he was one of just two linemen to pass the conditioning test.

Example 2:

Top rugby players in Australia do two activities for general endurance: The first is walking with a backpack for long distance, and the second is overland skiing. Both are successful.

Example 3:

We trained the third-ranked Olympic tri-athlete female on a non-motorized treadmill for a warm up, letting the heart rate go to 150-155 beats per minute (bpm). Then, immediately after, she would walk with a weight sled loaded to 45 pounds for the first week, for a distance of one to two and one-half miles, not letting the heart rate exceed 185 bpm. The second week, she would walk with 70 pounds for the same distance, with the same warm up and heart rate limit. On week three, her sled weight was 80 pounds for the same distance with the same warm up and heart rate limit at the two and one-half mile mark. Week four was a repeat of week one, with the addition of two and one-half miles on each proceeding week. The results were that she was constantly running, swimming, and biking faster. Other warm-ups would be 100 reps with a 65-pound bar.

In the beginning of training, her one rep max was 100 pounds. As training went on, her max grew to 145 pounds and her 100 rep max was 85 pounds. Other methods used were walking in a Westside Belt Squat machine for up to 25 miles with 90 pounds for great endurance, for three sets with a five-mile rest interval.

Example 4:

For short sprints of 60 meters to 100 meters and 200 meters, two high school girls would walk for 60 seconds with 450 pounds and three-minute rest intervals. One girl, 17-years-old, was capable of a 50½-inch box jump. Her 17-year-old training partner was capable of reducing her 60 meter time from 7.80 to 7.24. Note, when powerwalking, the time it takes to cover the distance—meaning 60 meters to 800 meters and so forth—should last at least that time. Always try to reduce the time, but with the same style of powerwalking. Rest intervals should be sufficient enough to fully recover from the exercises, meaning powerwalking or very high repetition squatting or belt squatting. Everyone will recover at their own rate. Do not sit down, but rather do some form of active rest, like jogging or walking. This will reduce mental fatigue and increase blood circulation.

There are many methods to increase endurance:

Repetitive Training

Here one trains one exercise with the same weight, which means a set intensity.
Example 1:

One may squat to a box for five minutes nonstop. One may set on the box for a few seconds. Or, do some Goodmornings, seated or standing. Do standing calf raises or hold a position at one-third or one-half squat. But most continue moving at the end of five minutes.

Example 2:

Power clean then drop to a front squat. Push jerk and drop weight to back in order to back squat. Then, push press from behind head. And so forth for three to five minutes.

Overhead Press

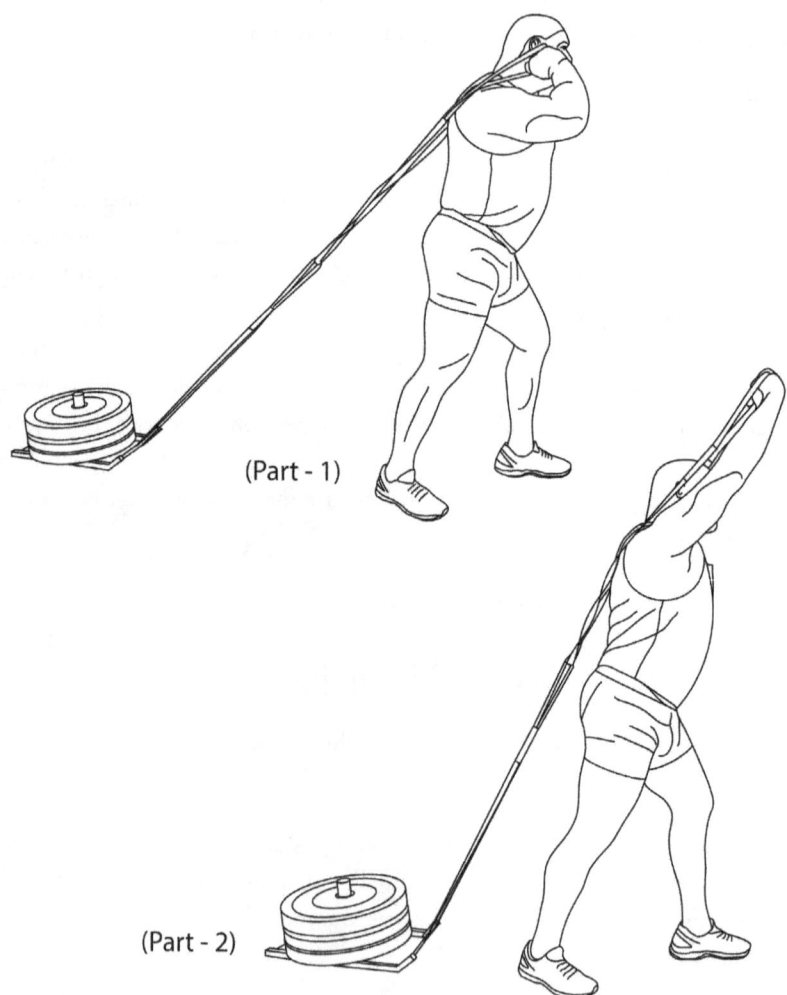

(Part - 1)

(Part - 2)

Fig. –Overhead shoulder presses using sled as a repetitive method

Pull Through

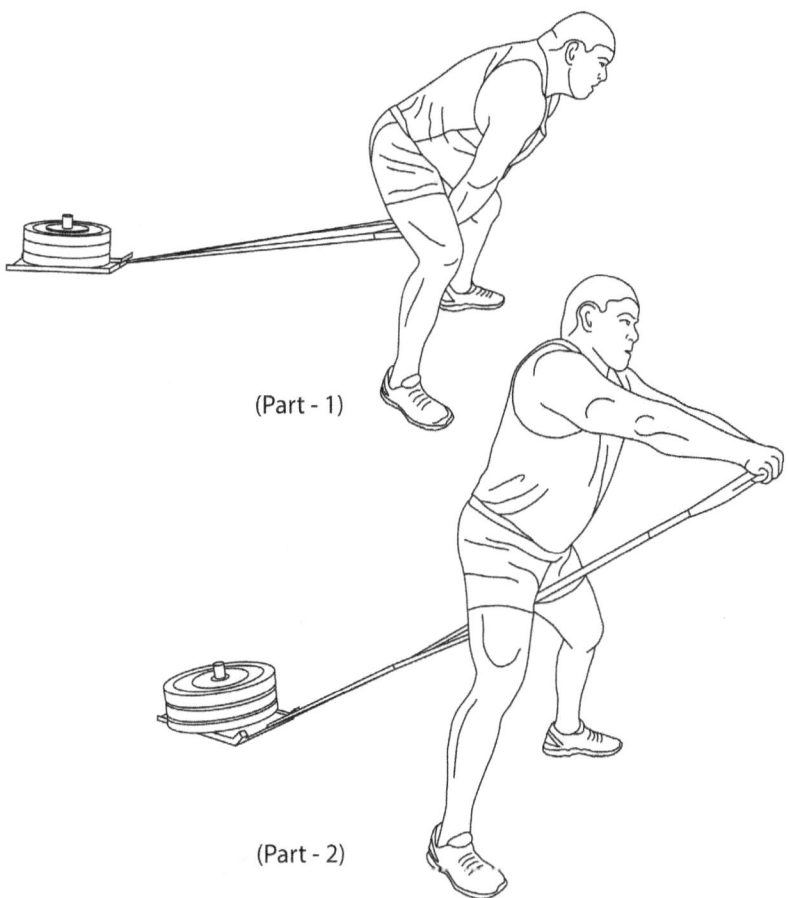

Fig. Pull throughs using sled as a repetitive method

Back Row

Fig. Back rows using sled as a repetitive method

Peck Deck Action

(Part - 1)

(Part - 2)

Fig. Chest flyes using sled as a repetitive method

Biceps Curl

(Part - 1)

(Part - 2)

Fig. Biceps curl using sled as a repetitive method

Triceps Extension

(Part 1)

(Part 2)

Fig. Triceps extension using sled as a repetitive method

Circuit Training

Circuit training can be many things. For most, it is using several exercises and rotating from one to another with a set rest interval or without a rest between sets. It is used for general endurance mainly during a general preparation phase. Do not use the same rest intervals all the time, rather make some shorter and others slightly longer. Greater endurance is increased by less rest. Keep in mind that the purpose of the circuits are to improve aerobic, power, muscle endurance, or cardiovascular endurance. Even flexibility, agility or speed can be performed.

Continuous with Variable Intensity

Example 1:

Walk on a non-motorized treadmill with 10-pound ankle weights plus a 30-pound weight vest with rubber bands attached to the ankles. After a set time, remove ankle weights and continue for a second set time interval. Then, remove the weight vest and finish walking or running.

Example 2:

Resistance jumping. Choose a box height to jump on to, then choose one to three forms of resistance such as ankle weights, a Kettlebell, or weight vest. Set a goal of 100 jumps for a set time. Start jumping with ankle weights, then remove after athlete starts to break form and continue until reaching the set goal. Two or three forms of resistance can be used, eliminating one at a time until reaching goal.

Example 3:

This system can also be done with sled walking by reducing some weight at a set distance. Remove when 400 meters is reached, then continue until signs of form breaking down appear. The same can also be done with cycling or swimming, to increase time or distance for endurance. For speed strength use the time of the event to increase speed.

High altitude training is always recommended for further endurance when normal training slows. The track coach must never stop learning more about track and field events constantly, but also a coach must understand the athlete he or she is in charge of. It is the coach's job to further the athlete's career, but to do so in the safest manor possible.

To learn more on these topics, use the following books:
Science of Sports Training by Thomas Kurz, 2001.
Pose Method of Running by Nicholas Romanov, PhD, 2002.
Explosive Power and Jumping Ability by Tadeusz Starzynski and Henryk Soazanski, PhD, 1995.
Supertraining by Mel Siff, Sixth Edition, 2003.
Science and Practice of Strength Training by V.M. Zatsioksky, Second Edition, 1995.
Underground Secrets to Faster Running by Barry Ross, 2005.
This is just a small list of books the author has gained knowledge from, along with many others listed at the end of the book that I have studied for more than 30 years.

STRENGTH ENDURANCE

Strength-endurance for running or recurring activity like rowing, multi-jumping and other must be trained with a light weight that one is capable of repeating for high reps, sometimes 100 reps per set with a predetermined rest interval. It is common for Westside to have a runner or sprinter do 60 reps in 60 seconds with the rest interval pre-set depending on the length of the event.

MMA fighter, Dan Gable, made famous five-minute dumbbell sets while sitting down. Another option is box squatting for five minutes while sitting, standing or bending over continuously.

V. Alexiev, the famous weightlifter from the former Soviet Union, would do a continuous set of combining all aspects of the clean or snatch without putting down the barbell. This would mean cleaning, then do a squat into a push press, drop down onto his back to do a Goodmorning and then back squat in any combinations for one to three minutes.

Anatoly Pisarenko, Alexiev's predecessor would do a similar style for strength-endurance to insure a higher work capacity to increase his training volume. His best snatch was 206 kilograms; CJ 265 kilograms in 1984; best 465 kilograms total. Thirteen total world records were trained at the world famous Dynamo club in Kiev. By the way, Alexiev made an incredible 80 all-time world records.

These are just a few examples where an athlete produced the same effort without decline in equal force development over a long period.

DYNAMIC ENDURANCE

Dynamic endurance is a somewhat different type of endurance as one must use many repetitions that include much higher muscular tension with both slow speed movements as well as fast speed-strength activities such as those you experience from playing ball sports where one goes from a slow pace to a sprint. MMA also is a fine example of changing pace from fast to slow and back again as well as moderate.

Dynamic endurance calls for exercising for long periods. As one chooses their sport and activity regarding the muscular tension involved—being tennis or weightlifting—close attention must be paid to the percent of a one rep max. A higher percent of a one rep max would be where greater muscle tension is needed by weights over 75 percent to 80 percent. At these percentages, these weights will only produce strength rather than endurance due to the athlete not being able to do high enough reps. If too many reps with weights at 70 percent to 85 percent are done it may increase too much hypertrophy resulting in less endurance due to the athlete having to carry excessive muscle mass.

The Westside system raises maximal strength levels by doing one rep on ME day. For speed strength, the percent is 75 percent to 80 percent to 85 percent in a three-week wave. Mostly at two reps. This is only speed strength due to the acceleration phase. The hypertrophy work is done only to the body parts that need it.

General Endurance

For building strength and general endurance for running any distance, one must power walk with a weight sled in many forms. For 60 meter to 100 meter and 200 meter sprints, use a sled loaded with body weight. This weight combination will increase the athlete's force production. This is not running, but power walking.

The method is a long and fast stride and the heels will touch the surface. This builds the entire group of running muscles. For sprints up to 200 meters, track time with more than one weight. For longer times like 400 meter and 800 meter, pull sled for time not distance. Example: A female 800-meter runner will cover 400 meters in about the same time they cover their 800-meter run. Women use a 20 kilogram sled for distances over 200 meters. Men use a 30 kilogram to 50 kilogram sled.

Pull a weight sled while carrying a medicine ball 20 meters to 60 meters. For general endurance, pull or push a wheelbarrow up to 800 meters. This will also help with balance. Walk or run on a non-motorized treadmill. Don't forget jumping rope. Some may use a heavy rope where strength is a factor in your sport.

Walk with ankle weights plus weight vest while carrying Kettlebells for up to two miles. Change the methods for developing general endurance. Hit a bag, swim or play sports in a team setting.

Being good at endurance or having great muscular endurance is being good at doing very little. If one has fast-twitch fiber then great endurance is hard to develop. Fast-twitch fiber contracts very hard as it has a much smaller amount of oxygen to sustain continuous work. It has been shown that mechanical work forced by stretching a contracted muscle is less in a muscle with mostly twitch fibers. This is due to the fact that the amount of stored elastic energy is greater in fast twitch. Simply said, know your fiber type from doing different sports to see what you will excel in. Fiber type is explained in great detail on Page 41 of *Supertraining* (2003) 6th Edition.

GENERAL ENDURANCE TRAINING

Thomas Kurz defines general endurance as the ability to effectively perform any non sport-specific effort for a prolonged time.

For a long-distance runner, general endurance is the ability to perform any exercise of low intensity and long duration while using almost all of the muscles of the body, including the upper body as well. This is based on aerobic fitness. If one only performs the type of endurance that is required for the sports task, or sport-specific endurance, they will suffer from accommodation. This is considered a general law of biology, where repeating the same sports activity, there will constantly be diminishing returns. This is according to V. M. Zatsiorsky in *The Science and Practice of Strength Training* (p. 5). Sport-specific endurance training is too often just doing the sport events themselves.

This will undoubtedly lead to accommodation. Westside uses the Conjugate System training for all sports. All special strengths are measured in time. By doing a very heavy low squat, that is moving very slow, for a longer time than it takes to do a new max squat, you will succeed in breaking your personal best.

Now, let's look at Westside's methods of directed endurance training for distance runners. This training system is designed to build not only the largest muscle groups, but also the smallest muscles that contribute in some small way to gain endurance and run at a faster pace for a prolonged period of time.

A female, 26-years-old, had an 800 meter time of 2.14 for six years. She came to Westside for nine weeks and ran a 2.04 800 meter. Here is how: For the first three weeks she did powerwalking for 60 meters, for 10 to 15 trips, with 135 pounds at a bodyweight of 125 pounds. Additionally, she did extensive walking in the belt squat machine, glute-hams, inverse hamstring work, reverse hypers, standing leg curls, and 200 reps of leg curls a day with 10-pound ankle weights. In the fourth week, she did powerwalking in a powerful manner for 400 meters.

Her initial time was 2.46 seconds. After nine weeks, her time was 2.14 seconds. She trained using a lightweight sled with 65 pounds for six trips in the first week, 55 pounds for six trips in the second week, and 45 pounds for six trips the third week. In the fourth week, the weight swings back to 65 pounds for six trips, 55 pounds in the fifth week, and 45 pounds in the sixth. Then again back up to 65 pounds on week seven, and 55 pounds on week eight. On week nine, for the six trips, she instead ran.

For a longer distance up to a 5K and 10K, one can pull a sled for 20 to 40 minutes, or at least the time it takes the individual to run the race. One must use a weight that does not cause the athlete to stagger left or right or cause one to lean forward excessively. It is recommended to do heavy, meaning at least bodyweight, weight sled pulls for 60 minutes. Start very powerfully on the heels to help develop the running muscles. One time per week, this is best done on a Monday, soon after racing. On Wednesday, use 25 pounds for women, and 45 pounds for men, to begin.

Do not forget the word optimal. Optimal is not under training or overtraining, but rather the correct amount of training. While one must train or exercise through fatigue to gain greater endurance, training must stop when form starts to become distorted. The optimal starting weight should be 25 pounds for women and 45 pounds for men when doing interval training.

According to Mel Siff in *Supertraining*, interval training calls for a runner to use loads of low to medium intensity for a set working time limit with a predetermined rest period or rest interval to recover. As one adapts to more strenuous training the rest intervals must stay the same. Or, to make training more difficult, shorten the rest intervals periodically.

For example, one who can complete a half marathon in 90 minutes can pull a sled for three trips of 30 minutes, with a rest interval to reduce heart rate 75 percent or under. Then, proceed with a second trip. Use the same interval for the third trip as well, as your sled pull times come down, meaning you are covering more distance in the 30-minute work interval. As you work, capacity grows. The working intervals can grow to 45 minutes. This means you are now doing just two working intervals of 45 minutes, instead of three at 30 minutes. Your work capacity has now grown considerably. Remember to use a slightly different weight each week during a three-week wave.

A second example would be a three-hour marathon runner may start with six 30-minute intervals with a rest interval that permits one to recover to at least 75 percent of their resting heart rate. As his or her work capacity increases, the 30-minute sled pull intervals should increase to 45 minutes with the same rest intervals, or shorter if possible. After finding a 45-minute work interval comfortable, increase the sled work to 60 minutes. This is very possible during a yearly plan to work towards a goal of two 90-minute work intervals.

Remember, use one amount of weight per week. There are many different waves to choose from. First, add weight each week for three weeks. This is an example of a three-week wave. Second, start with the heaviest sled weight; say 55 pounds for week one, 45 pounds for week two, and 35 pounds for week three. The wave must fit your personality. It is important to change the intensity or weight each week. The weight sled is low-low intensity to develop endurance while working through fatigue. By doing so, endurance increases.

To develop endurance, there must be many types of work done. Not only walking with a weight sled, but also work on a non-motorized treadmill, high repetition belt squatting or barbell squatting can also be introduced into the training program. Running up and down hills, running in sand, or any high altitude for interval training with a weight sled should be kept at subcritical intensity. Subcritical intensity is when the demand for oxygen is below the lactate threshold.

While walking with bodyweight is of small benefit to endurance, Westside has had great results with heavy resistance walking. Heavy resistance walking has a far greater effect on the respiratory and cardiovascular systems, which results in running better. But it means using a weight vest of 50 pounds to 100 pounds, plus five-pound to 10-pound ankle weights, while carrying four kilogram to eight kilogram Kettlebells and walking from one-half mile up to five miles for those who have a very high level of endurance and an ability to recover from a high volume of low intensity work.

Here are some signs of not recovering, or overtraining:

- Becoming injured
- Feeling constant fatigue both physically and mentally
- Getting sick often
- Wanting stimulants, like energy drinks or sweets
- Having a hard time getting up or wanting to stay in bed late

For females, another sign is getting PMS-like symptoms. This happens when one does too little aerobic exercises compared to anaerobic exercises, according to Maffetone, 1994, (p. 201) *Science of Sports Training* by Thomas Kurz.

CHAPTER 7

CONJUGATE SEQUENCE SYSTEM

Before detailing the Conjugate System by Westside Barbell, it is to your interest to see a block-style periodization that is divided into three blocks during the year. As mentioned earlier, the author strongly disagrees with the block-style training programs.

- First phase—accumulation. This block is a wide base of special strength and special exercises. The athlete performs a high volume of training with a work load aimed at increasing speed of movements. Science refers to this speed as individually stable speed.
- Second phase—intensification. The training shifts to sport-specific exercises that are close to the form of movements for that specific sport while attempting to increase speed of movements. This cannot be maintained for long periods of time. And one must use longer rest intervals. The more advanced athlete can prolong the intensification block by shorting the accumulation block phase.
- Third phase—transformation. This phase takes advantage of the first two phases and aims at bringing forth the athletes highest sports results during the peaking phase that lasts a short time.

In the Westside Conjugate System, once an athlete masters his or her events the need for a accumulation phase should not be repeated. This means the athlete should not detrain to the point of starting over the process completely, but each proceeding season the level of preparedness is higher.

The author's Conjugate method builds all special strengths at the same time while raising the weak muscle groups to improve running form. This calls for four weight-training workouts per week, two for upper body, and two for lower body. As one becomes stronger, the speed strength ability is maintained by a three-week pendulum wave with explosive strength trained by jumping or training with 30 percent to 40 percent where movement velocity is fast. Speed strength is trained at 75 percent, 80 percent, and 85 percent in a three-week pendulum wave at intermediate velocity. Strength speed is developed on max effort day, where motion velocity is slow. One must think of a shot putter's training. They constantly try to become stronger and faster even though a shot put weight is always 16 pounds. This means all strengths must be trained together. And the same holds true for a runner. The Conjugate System calls for special exercises to be close in nature to the classical five lifts. This includes rack or box pulls, rack or box squats, high snatch, or clean pulls. But also, sprinting shorter or longer distances than the athlete's special events that he or she competes in. The Conjugate System uses small special exercises to bring up a lacking muscle group to perfect form. It utilizes isometric work with zero or little motion to allow the coach to check form at precise angles of the motion in its interoperability. Everything must be connected somehow or the system will fail. Small exercises are set into groups of three or four and rotated as often as necessary to avoid the Law of Accommodation completely. To adapt to a training program is never to adapt. We have talked about special exercises. Large special exercises meaning with a barbell, and small special exercises meaning with a dumbbell or some amount of body resistance or a special device or machine. Don't forget the loading for the athlete, meaning volume and intensity zones, as well as restoration methods.

Let's look at an explosive, or speed strength, training day. For the lower body, or running muscles, this means high volume and moderate intensity. Sometimes ten sets of two reps for speed strength and ten sets of as high as five reps for explosive strength. This day builds acceleration or a fast rate of force development. This system also is used for any style of pressing. Seventy-two hours later a max effort workout must be done to coincide with the high volume day.

The max effort workout is much lower volume. This is due to working up to a one rep max as fast as possible. This keeps the volume low, but by making a new PR (personal record), the intensity is as high as possible, meaning over 100 percent. Both days the total volume is 80 percent of special exercises and 20 percent is made up with a barbell exercise to include the five classical exercises: squat, bench, deadlift, clean or snatch. It is very important to rotate from high volume to low volume and from low-moderate intensity to low intensity. This will ensure one does not experience accommodation. Yes, it can happen, not only with exercises but with the workload and their intensities. Remember, every aspect of training must be connected including restoration, which includes sleep and eating properly. Remember, not to plan is a plan to fail.

ACCOMODATING RESISTANCE

With submaximal loads Westside uses accommodating resistance (AR) methods with chains or bands. The reason we use AC is to develop maximal tension throughout the entire range of motion. Machines have been developed for years to provide resistance. Nautilus exercise machines introduced in 1970 came to the author's mind along with its founder Arthur Jones, but Dr. Jonas Zander first used this concept in the late 1800s. Dr Zander's exercise machine won a gold medal at the 1876 Centennial Exhibition in Philadelphia. We have learned over the years that a machine can build muscle, but not motion. When attaching chains to a barbell for AC, the athlete must not only control the barbell, but also keep the bands in control at the same time. While many machines say they are for AC, they are not made correctly and do not match the human strength curve, but bands and chains do so perfectly. When using just barbell weight, it can be heavy to start at the bottom, and with just bands it can be too light at the bottom due to band shrinkage.

COMBINATIONS OF RESISTANCE METHODS

A barbell alone will have a deceleration phase due to the lack of human leverage. The addition of bands or chains to the bar will eliminate deceleration almost completely. But, a second bonus is providing an overspeed eccentrics phase that causes a greater stretch reflex, which is a major factor in minimal ground contact.

The three factors to running faster is the fastest minimal ground contact and how much muscular force one can apply during ground contact, plus how often you touch the track during a race. AC is the most effective method to increase explosive speed and absolute strength. One must overcome gravity vertically. It is 90 percent of the effort to run down a track while only 10 percent effort is applied to go horizontally down the track. This is why correct weight training is so important for running. After perfecting running form, the major task is to become more powerful. Take a look at the basic physics that prove this point. Work is defined as the product of the net force and displacement through which force is exerted, or $W=Fd$. Secondly, let's look at power. Power is defined as work done divided by the time used to do the work, or $P=W/T$. This means if two sprinters are to race, the more powerful one will do the work in less time. Work meaning the distance ran. A coach may not agree, but, physics is physics.

BAND TENSION

For explosive strength, use 30 percent of a one rep max with bar weight plus 25 percent band tension at lockout. Note, there must be band tension at the start of all lifts. The sets can be eight to 10, with the reps per set ranging from three to 10. The last rep should be just as fast as the first rep on all sets. This can depend on the level of preparedness of the athlete. Use a three-week pendulum wave with 30 percent for week one, 35 percent for week two, and 40 percent for week three. Then, wave back to week one and start over using a different bar, stance, grip, or starting position. Your front, back, and overhead squats will all have a different max to arrive at what percentage to use.

SPEED STRENGTH

Load the bar to 50 percent, 55 percent, and 60 percent, with 25 percent band tension at the top. This will build acceleration to the completion of the lift. The start of the race calls for explosive strength. Explosive strength is the ability to rapidly increase force (Tidow), the steeper the increase of strength in time, the greater the explosive strength. The acceleration phase is due to speed strength, which is responsible for maintaining top speed while sprinting. We know as loads grow larger, force becomes greater and motion velocity decreases as external resistance increases. To learn more, look at the relationship between force and velocity, or Hill's equation for muscle contraction in *Supertraining*, 2003, Sixth Edition, p. 145. The sets and reps are eight to 12 sets with three to four reps per set. Never exceed four reps or bar speed will suffer.

STRENGTH SPEED

To build absolute strength use a combination of 50 percent band tension of your one rep max plus barbell weight. For example, for a 500-pound squat max use 250 pounds of band tension on the bar first, and then start adding weight. Try to reach a top weight by doing two sets of two reps then three singles. This is from the data of Aspruplin, 1974, found in *Managing the Training of Weightlifters*, p. 32. Data from speed strength comes from the findings of 780 skilled weight lifters from the extensive work of A. D. Ermakov and N. S. Atanasov. For research the author followed the experimentations of Y. V. Verkhoshansky and Westside Barbell's work with 77 men who had an official squat of 800 pounds to 1,210 pounds. The author is also credited with developing the combinations of resistance methods training starting in 1990. Find more in *Supertraining 2003, Sixth Edition*, p. 409.

Remember, with the fastest barbell speed, explosive strength is developed. At intermediate barbell speed, speed strength is built. Also, as the barbell speed slows to near zero velocity, speed strength is measured best. Absolute strength is measured at isometric conditions.

CHAPTER 8

Foundation of Special Strength

Strength Speed

Strength speed is defined by low velocity training. It must be used in sports that require great strength. Weightlifting, powerlifting and shot put come to mind. These sports require great speed by greater strength. This strength is best trained by the maximal effort method or M-E training. This method is best for improving both intermuscular and intramuscular coordination. It is important to know that the central nervous system (CNS) and the muscles adapt only to the load placed upon them. Low velocity training will bring about the greatest strength gains due to the maximal number of muscle units (MU) that are used and their optimal discharge frequency.

The Westside system does not call for heavy efforts of 90 percent and close to 100 percent, but rather recommends working up to an all-time record each week. This can be done by selecting a special pull, press, or squat and choosing a new special pull, press or squat each week.

Scientific studies have shown that training the same exercise for three weeks at 90 percent or greater will stop progress. This is the Law of Accommodation. Avoiding accommodation calls for choosing a pull that is close in coordination with the lift you are trying to improve on. It means using the Conjugate System.

For example, for the deadlift do a rack pull at three different starting points. Or deadlift from a one-inch, two-inch, or four-inch box.

For combinations of resistance method use band tension on platform of 220 pounds or 280 pounds depending on your strength. Or rack pull with 170 pounds, 250 pounds or 350 pounds of tension plus weight. This system works for any of the five classical lifts.

Even running speed can stall. This is the so called Speed Barrier. Avoiding the speed barrier also calls for special exercises to replace much of the running. A different version of the conjugate system, just like speed strength, can be explained by the relationship between force and velocity. This is shown by the 1938 hyperbolic equation known as Hills Equation of Muscle Contraction. Hills equation says that motion velocity decreases as external load increases. Maximum Force (Fmm) is attained when velocity is small.

We all know that when a lift grows heavier the barbell moves slower until, finally, your force output is less than the weight on the bar and you cannot complete the lift.

Shock Method

Y.V. Verkhoshansky made the term "shock method" synonymous with the terms explosive-strength and reactive-ability by his conclusion that an athlete can jump off low boxes with an immediate rebound for a fast amortization phase. And, his work with jumping off higher boxes—42-inch and above—for absolute strength development due to a slower amortization phase. This, of course, is depth jumps.

But, there are many other methods that will force great stimulation to produce the highest level of functional adaptation. The following shock methods can also be referred to as maximal effort exercises.

Through scientific studies it was found that training the same stimulus for three weeks creates a detraining effect. This is the phenomenon of Accommodation. Through more than 40 years of research and using more than 100 of the highest skilled athletes and powerlifters the world has to offer, ways to combat accommodation are available.

We found that by using a special large barbell exercise each week, rotating to a different special barbell exercise the next week, powerlifters could lift not 90 percent, but 100 percent. They could make a new record each and every week year round with no signs of accommodation at all. Over 90 percent of the time they would also establish new records.

The author found like many before that progressive overloading will lead into periods of no improvement in speed or strength.

STRENGTH MANUAL FOR RUNNING

There are too many Westside M-E workouts to list, but this extensive list should help the coach or self-taught athlete to gain incredible strength.

Pulling Shock Methods

1. Rack pulls for deadlifting
2. Plates 2.5" off floor bar weight only
3. Plates 4.5" off floor bar weight only
4. Plates 6.5" off floor bar weight only
5. Plates 2.5" off floor bar weight plus 170 band tension
6. Plates 4.5" off floor bar weight plus 170 band tension
7. Plates 6.5" off floor bar weight plus 170 band tension
8. Plates 2.5" off floor bar weight plus 250 band tension
9. Plates 4.5" off floor bar weight plus 250 band tension
10. Plates 6.5" off floor bar weight plus 250 band tension
11. Plates 2.5" off floor bar weight plus 350 band tension
12. Plates 4.5" off floor bar weight plus 350 band tension
13. Plates 6.5" off floor bar weight plus 350 band tension
14. Deadlift off floor bar weight plus 220 band tension
15. Deadlift off floor bar weight plus 280 band tension
16. Deadlift standing on 2" box bar weight only
17. Deadlift standing on 4" box bar weight only
18. Deadlift with plates on 2" mat bar weight only
19. Deadlift with plates on 4" mat bar weight only

20. Deadlift standing on 2" box with 220 band tension

21. Deadlift standing on 4" box with 280 band tension

22. Deadlift with plates on 2" box with 220 band tension

23. Deadlift with plates on 4" box with 280 band tension

By alternating from sumo style to conventional the M-E efforts have doubled.

WEIGHTLIFTING STYLE PULLS

1. Power clean weight only
2. Power snatch weight only
3. Power clean weight plus 25% band tension
4. Power snatch weight plus 25% band tension
5. Power clean wide grip weight only
6. Power snatch close grip weight only
7. Power clean wide grip weight plus 25% band tension
8. Power snatch close grip weight plus 25% band tension
9. All clean standing on 2" box
10. All clean standing on 4" box
11. All clean at shin level
12. All clean at below knee level
13. All clean at above knee level
14. All clean at top of thigh
15. All snatch at shin
16. All snatch below knee

17. All snatch above knee

18. All snatch top of thigh

19. Muscle up clean

20. Muscle up snatch

21. Straight leg clean

22. Straight leg snatch

SPECIAL SQUATS FOR SHOCK METHODS

1. Back squat weight only
2. Front squat weight only
3. Back squat weight plus 70 pound band tension
4. Front squat weight plus 70 pound band tension
5. Back squat weight plus 140 pound band tension
6. Front squat weight plus 140 pound band tension
7. Back squat weight plus 250 pound band tension
8. Front squat weight plus 250 pound band tension
9. Overhead squat weight plus 70 pound band tension
10. Overhead squat weight plus 140 pound band tension
11. Overhead squat weight plus 250 pound band tension
12. Box squat weight only close stance
13. Box squat weight only wide stance
14. Box squat close weight plus 70 pounds
15. Box squat close weight plus 140 pounds

16. Box squat close weight plus 250 pounds

17. Box squat wide weight plus 170 pounds

18. Box squat wide weight plus 140 weight band tension

19. Box squat wide weight plus 250 weight band tension

20. Safety squat bar all varieties

21. Box bar all varieties

22. 14" cambered bar all varieties

For pulling and squatting there is a list of special barbell exercises to try a new record each week. A person has only so much maximum strength to develop, but by using band tension up to 700 lb or chain weight up to 500 lb or a combination of resistance, anyone's normal strength curve can change due to one particular biomechanical weakness or strength that we all possess.

PRESSING SHOCK METHODS

Here are 12 special lifts, but with two band tensions—say eight five and 125lbs —you have tripled the lift.

1. Benchpress (BP) close grip weight only

2. BP wide grip weight only

3. Incline press close grip weight only

4. Incline press wide grip weight only

5. Decline press close grip weight only

6. Decline press wide grip weight only

7. Standing press close grip weight only

8. Standing press wide grip weight only

9. Behind head press close grip weight only

10. Behind head press wide grip weight only

11. Seated press wide grip weight only

12. Seated press close grip weight only

Now the three jerks listed below can be nine separate lifts if two band tensions are implemented to the rotation. In a monthly rotation after selecting the special exercises that work best, jumping five pounds a month will lead to 60 percent a year.

1. Jerk

2. Push Jerk

3. Power Jerk

OTHER SHOCK METHODS

MAXIMAL ECCENTRICS

Lowering a weight larger than a lifter can raise concentrically. This builds absolute eccentric muscle tension.

OVERSPEED ECCENTRICS

This is performed by lowering a barbell as fast as possible, but under control. Through the experiment at Westside by the author it is best performed by only using 40 percent of one's potential eccentric and best achieved by using strong rubber bands. The bands reduce the load in the bottom to accommodate resistance eccentrically.

This style brings forth great reversible strength.

MAXIMUM ECCENTRICS

This is done by starting a lift without an eccentric phase first. There is no reversible strength to aid on the concentric action. A heavy load will build absolute strength. Light weight will build explosive power concentrically.

FORCED REPITITION

This is commonly used with light weights for hypertrophy or bodybuilding. It is done with the help of a spotter assisting on the final last few reps through the mini max.

RESTRICTED RANGE POWER BACK WORK

In restricted range power back work the athlete will push or pull weight from a lower pin to a higher pin a few inches apart for a set of repetitions or for one rep that is held for two to six seconds. This is referred to as the Hoffman Method.

Westside has four major workouts in a weekly plan: two for speed strength and two for M-E or shock method workouts. Remember each week a large special barbell workout is rotated to avoid accommodation. There are many such special barbell exercises to choose from, but the individual must choose which ones work best for them. He or she must also choose in what order they are rotated while far away from a meet as well as in the weeks approaching the competition.

Westside includes such M-E or shock training for everyone who trains at Westside from two Olympic Gold sprinters to a 70-foot 10-inch shot putter to a 10:17 collegiate sprinter and world record holders in powerlifting. The diverse list goes on and on. It must be noted that it includes 15-year-old boys who became world champions or all-time world record holders in the powerlifts at 20 years old. The method has also been used with great success for high school track girls who are 17 years old. The key is to first build a large base of General Physical Preparedness (GPP) with no injuries at all. The injuries come from too much running without a broad special strength base, not from the shock training.

With such extreme stimuli the volume should be monitored carefully as to not interfere with the high volume of speed or explosive strength on dynamic day or, 72 hours later, M-E or shock training day.

Isometric Strength

There are many pros and cons to consider when doing isometric training. It works to build voluntary strength maximally at the joint ankle where the exertion takes place.

Note: Other research has shown the effects of isometric training can stimulate strength 15 degrees in either direction. This explains why six positions are used in training.

There was an isometric craze in the mid-fifties. The famous York barbell company in York, Pa., headed by Bob Hoffman, the father of modern weight lifting, built a power rack just for isometric work. From front to back it was roughly 12-inches with two sets of pins. One would use the lower pin to have a starting position and push or pull into a second pin and exert maximum force for two to six seconds.

If one desires they can exert force for up to 10 seconds by not holding their breath. Yet other research has stated that the length of time one exerts is more effective than a maximal exertion. This could explain why wrestlers are so strong in the clench. This is a form of quasi isometrics.

When doing isometrics, the force should be slow until top force is developed. Its main purpose is to build absolute strength. It has never been determined whether dynamic or isometric work is best for strength, but the author believes for maximum strength development isometrics are superior. For the development of a fast movement, do a fast pull or push into a pin set six to eight inches above the starting pin, but hold for one second, then release and lower to the lower pin. Repeat for five to 10 reps raising strength as fast as possible. Use only the bar or a bar loaded with alternative weight. Use at a sticking point—the position where the resistance or muscle weakness can't be overcome—where ever it may occur.

Remember, it may bring greater results by holding tension for longer periods of time. The force velocity curve shows that as the weight or resistance grows to near max or max, the exertion becomes closer to isometric work. This happens at the sticking on the largest loads.

THE ADVANTAGES OF ISOMETRICS

1. Isometrics makes for easy observation for the coach to check form in various angles.

2. Little to no muscle mass increase.

3. A six-second contraction can cause the same positive effects as many ballistic contractions at maximal force at no more than 0.1 seconds.

4. Takes little to do a workout compared to weight training.

5. It's a simple system where all one needs is an unmovable bar in a rack or a barbell loaded to over a maximum of the individual strength protocol.

ISOMETRIC DISADVANTAGES

1. It is easy to fatigue the CNS. Also, it can have a harmful effect on the cardiovascular system.

2. Too much static work can reduce speed of movement and reduce coordination. Doing only isometrics or static work can cause you to lose the elasticity of the muscles.

We suggest not holding your breath while exerting max force and using longer rest intervals between sets and contractions. Above all, do not hold a contraction for longer than six seconds and most of the side effects can be avoided.

Reactive Methods

Depth jumps were made famous by Dr. Verkhoshansky. He found that potential energy changes to kinetic energy (KE) when an athlete's body free falls to the ground. The athlete builds reversible strength upon rebounding upward after striking the ground.

Watch as one drops a basketball onto the floor as fast as possible. It rebounds much higher. Why? The increase in velocity that causes greater KE. In slow motion the ball will flatten out upon contact causing deformation due to ground contact. This flattening upon ground contact also occurs when running at high speed as the soft tissue has deformation much like the ball. The greater the force on the ground in the minimal contact time, the greater the KE.

Combination Resistance Methods

One combination resistance method would be the weight-release system. For speed strength, one loads the barbell to 60 percent of a one rep max then adds 20 percent of your one rep max on the weight releaser. On the eccentric, you are then lowering a total of 80 percent upon the weight. Touching the ground the releasers fall off and you raise the 60 percent left on the bar.

For explosive strength, load the barbell to 30 percent of a one rep max and load the weight releaser with 30 percent of a one rep max. On the eccentric phase you will lower 60 percent with barbell weight and weight releaser weight combined. The weight releaser will unload 30 percent and the athlete will raise the remaining 30 percent as explosively as possible.

A breakaway parachute is another example of a contrast method. Do several box jumps with 10-pound ankle weights or Kettlebells then remove the ankles and jump with just bodyweight. Or, work up to a Kettlebell weight of 15 kilograms to 30 kilograms for a few sets. Then, use just bodyweight to jump to a new personal record.

Heavy-Light System for Explosive Power

Do a few sets of one to two reps at 90 percent plus then reduce weight to 30 percent of a one rep max and do a series of explosive squat jumps, pulls or presses. Some of the many proven methods of combination of resistance made popular by the author are adding chains hanging from a barbell and using rubber bands to a loaded barbell as well as using both band tension and chain weight to the barbell.

RESULTS OF AN 18-MONTH EXPERIMENT

Westside performed an 18-month experiment with top-10 ranked squatters. The subjects used the M-E method once a week on Monday. Here only barbell weight was used. Everyone worked up to a new record on a special barbell exercise at over 90 percent success rate, followed by a very high volume of special exercise, mostly small exercises.

The Westside volume for an 800-pound squat is 9,000 pounds. This is only 20 percent of the total volume on speed strength day. Three subjects used three, three-week waves where the bar weight was 400 pounds on week one, 440 pounds on week two and 480 pounds on week three. The first three-week wave added 80 pounds of chain. The second three-week wave added 120 pounds of chain. The third three-week wave used 160 pounds of chain.

The circa-max day was 21 days out from meet with de-loading for the next 14 days. One subject's previous squat was 760-760-770. On meet day, each made an 804-pound squat record. This system made progress for 18 months along with several other members, then the results were recorded in *Powerlifting USA*.

Chains attached to the bar provided accommodating resistance. The barbell was loaded to 50 to 55 and 60 percent in a three-week pendulum wave. The chains do not affect speed on the eccentric phase. Band tension added to barbell, barbell plus band tension. After 20 years of experimenting with the following band tension percentages for the development of a particular strength.

The Combination for Explosive Strength

Load bar to 25 percent of a one rep max plus 25 percent band tension at top of lift. This will increase explosive strength by accommodating resistance. The true value, however, is providing and adding an overspeed eccentric phase. This will provide a virtual force effect in the bottom—a force that is present, but not recognized.

One must use the optimal amount of eccentric strength, which is 40 percent of your eccentric strength. Remember the experiment with the basketball with a falling speed of 9.8m/s? Think of it as the speed of acceleration of gravity near the surface of Earth versus a higher speed downward by throwing the basketball to the ground. You can also think of it as dropping a rock to the ground and that rock racing a rock covering the same distance shot downward by a sling shot. Why is overspeed eccentrics important to reversal strength? It creates KE.

While reading *Supertraining*, the author came across a segment entitled "Kinetic Energy and Strength Processes." The segment referred to a barbell that fell from a predetermined height causing some velocity by falling. Then the athlete's task was to stop it from falling and to quickly thrust it upward. This action changes the kinetic energy of the falling barbell and is transformed during the catching or amortization phase into the athlete's elastic energy. The faster the switching phase the greater the amount of muscular force that is developed. The *Supertraining* segment brought up a larger question: What and how can one increase the rate of speed during the eccentric phase? The answer is rubber band tension.

For the development of speed strength, you need the combination of resistance methods. This is a case of variable resistance training. The following chart was developed after researching at least 75 cases of men who squat 800 pounds or more under the guidance of Westside Barbell. The chart illustrates the proper combination of barbell weight plus band tension.

Bar speed .8m/s 400lb Max

	Bar weight	Band T	Sets	Reps	Volume	
Week 1	200	25%	12	2	4800	50%
Week 2	220	25%	12	2	5680	55%
Week 3	240	25%	10	2	4800	60%

Bar speed .8m/s 600lb Max

	Bar weight	Band T	Sets	Reps	Volume	
Week 1	300	25%	12	2	7200	50%
Week 2	330	25%	12	2	8520	55%
Week 3	360	25%	10	2	7200	60%

As you can see, the common denominator is the bar speed. The total percent at the top is 75 percent, 80 percent and 85 percent. This is mechanical power. It is achieved at intermediate range of velocity and power. It is explained in more detail in *Science and Practice of Strength Training*, Second Edition.

These three percentages (75, 80, 85) of a one rep max that Westside provides the athlete as the most appropriate intensity is used for 50 percent of all training for the high skilled lifter based on the 1995 data of A.D. Ermakov and N.S. Atanasov for the snatch and clean. But it does not matter what lift is used. What is important is the percent of a one rep max and the bar speed it is trained at.

Just as important is the research by A.S. Prilepin in 1974, which established that when training at 70 percent after six reps the bar speed was reduced causing less force development. This holds true that a loss of force was found for 80 percent above four reps and 90 percent after two reps. To learn more read *Managing the Training of Weightlifters*, 1982.

There is a common misconception that a weight lifter does not have to be strong. If one looks at a 60-kilogram weightlifter with a clean of 195 kilograms, his first pull is 1.2 to 1.4m/s and his explosive segment is roughly 2.2 to 2.4m/s. Now, let's look at a SHW with a clean of 250 kilograms. His first pull is basically the same as the second pull. You must surely realize that the 60-kilogram lifter is not strong enough to lift the 250 kilograms.

As weights grow larger the bar speed will decrease. This is basic physics. This brings us to why does the SHW lift a larger weight at the same speed the 60-kilogram lifter does? Answer: the SHW possesses a much higher level of absolute strength.

This special strength is referred to as Slow Strength. Here the bar speed is much due to the large loads that must be lifted. With just barbell weight there is a problem. The weight can be too heavy to lift to the top position; or in benching or squatting after the eccentric phase, the barbell is too heavy to return to the top concentrically.

If one was to use just band tension, the band tension at the top would be great, but too light in the bottom due to band shrinkage. So, how can one have a maximum load at the top and bottom of the lift? A combination of bar weight plus bands. During a nine-week experiment with a circa max phase where A.J. Roberts made a parallel box squat with 740 pounds of barbell weight, plus 440 pounds of band tension, the bar speed was .5m/s. The total load equals 1180 pounds.

During the nine-week experiment, A.J. also made 700 pounds of band tension and 510 pounds of barbell weight equally 1,210 pounds. At the contest that followed the experiment, A.J. officially squatted 1,205 pounds with the 700 pounds of band tension and 510 pounds of barbell weight. The bar speed was closer to .5m/s.

By using two different barbell weights and band tension combinations, we made this discovery: as one only has one maximal lift, it can be done by changing the strength curve causing the body to respond to different rates of speed by placing the maximum resistance at different points during the lift.

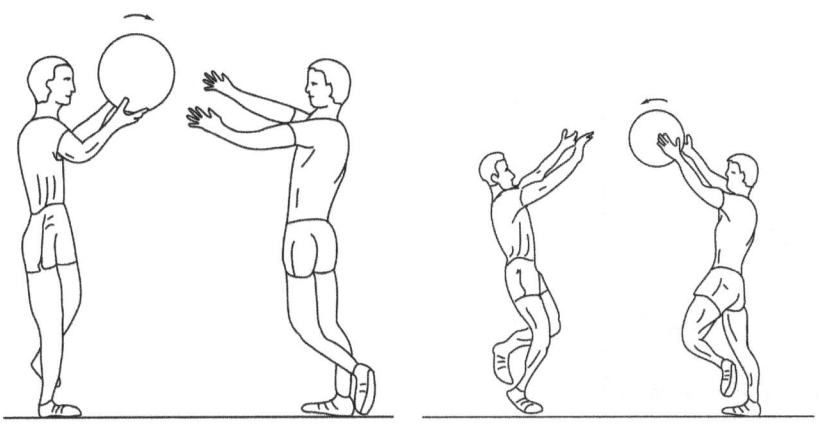

Fig. Single leg standing medicine ball pass

Fig. Single leg standing medicine ball toss

Fig. Medicine ball passes while jumping.

Fig. Single leg medicine ball forward toss

Fig. Squat Jump med ball toss

Fig. Medicine ball toss from bend over position.

Fig. Single leg takeoff overhead med ball toss

Fig. Med ball rotational toss

Fig. Med ball overhead toss

Fig. Jumping med ball throws to the front

Fig. Med ball throws with the ball on the ground. Lift the ball from the ground and jump in the air with double leg takeoff while throwing the ball up.

Fig. Deep squat med ball throws

Fig. (Left) Med ball passes using hands with ball rolling on the ground. (Right) med ball pass using feet as in soccer

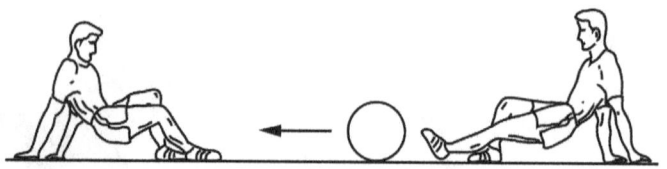

Fig. Med ball pass using single leg

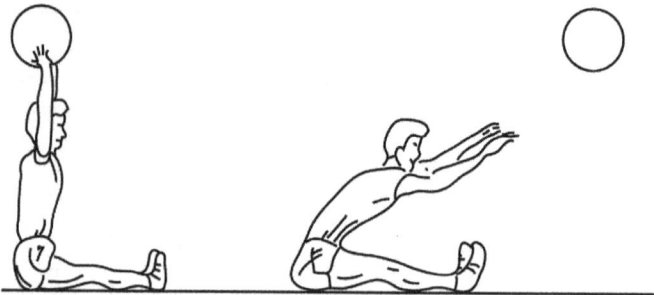

Fig. Sit-up med ball throws

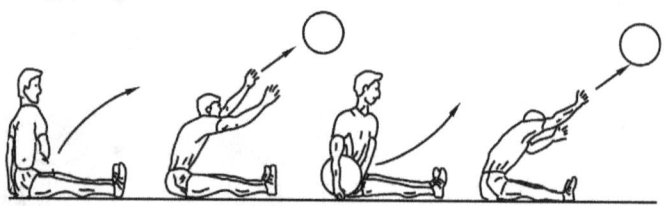

Fig. Seated med ball side throws.

Fig. A variation of sit-up med ball throws with a bend at the hips entire time.

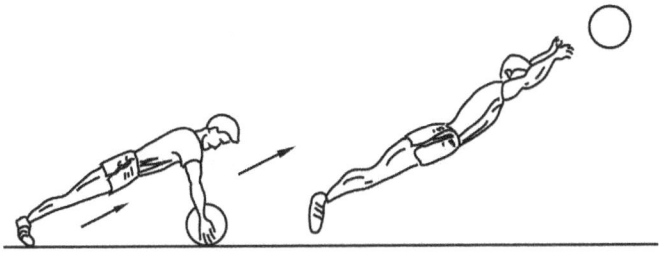

Fig. Med ball throw with takeoff from the plank position.

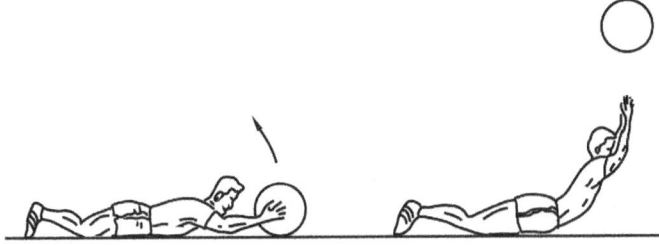

Fig. Hyper extension med ball backward toss

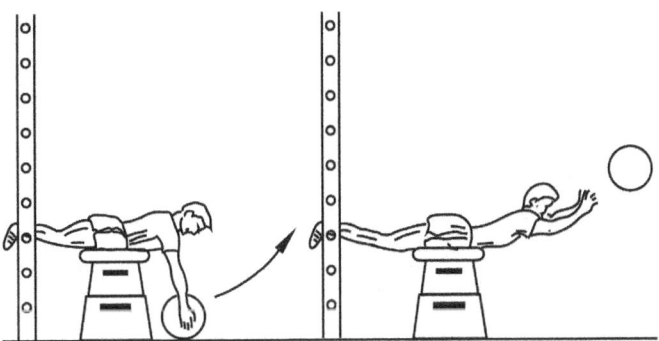

Fig. Full extension superman med ball toss

Fig. Kneeling med ball toss

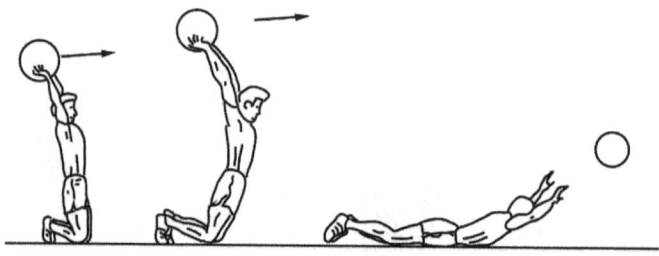

Fig. Kneeling overhead med ball throws

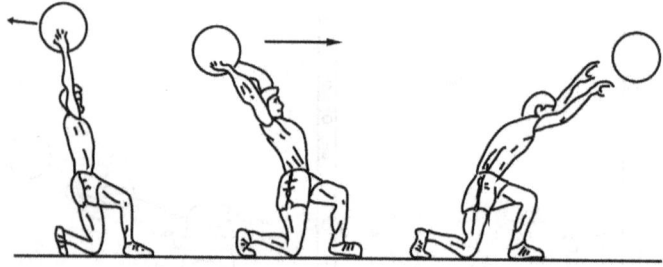

Fig. Lunge overhead med ball forward throw

STRENGTH MANUAL FOR RUNNING

Fig. Med ball kick to the partner's chest

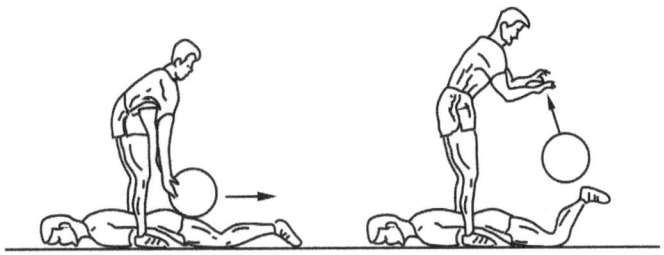

Fig. Lying med ball hamstring kick

Fig. Seated med ball quadriceps kick

Fig. Seated med ball quadriceps rebound kick.

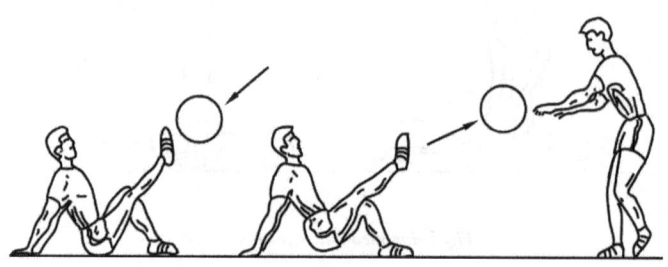

Fig. Seated med ball one leg quadriceps kick

Fig. Seated Hip extension med ball kick

Fig. Lying med ball quadricep rebound.

Fig. Lying med ball single leg quadricep rebound

Fig. Seated leg extension med ball rebound with support

Fig. Seated leg extension med ball rebound without support

Fig. Seated single leg extension med ball rebound without support

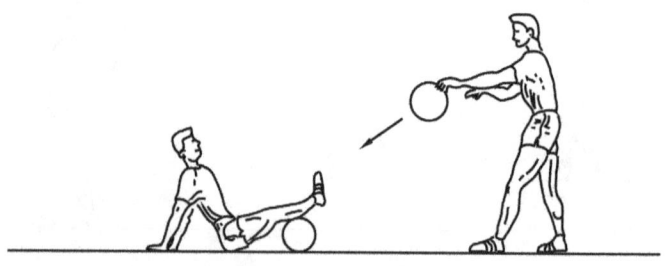

Fig. Double leg med ball catch with support

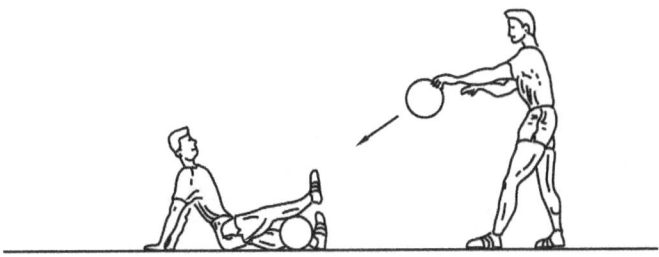

Fig. Single leg med ball catch with support

Fig. Double leg med ball catch without support

Fig. Single leg med ball catch without support

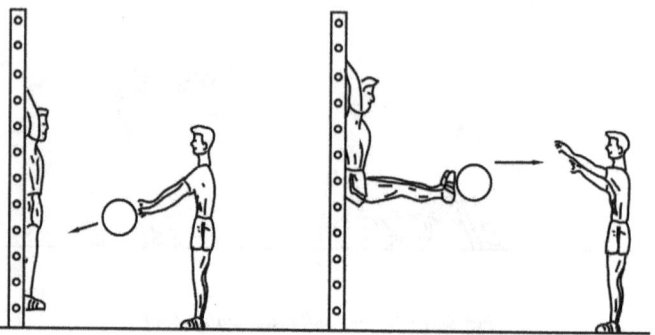

Fig. Hanging double leg med ball rebound

Fig. Hanging single leg med ball rebound

CHAPTER 9

Circa Max Chart

Circa max band tension is slightly over or under 40 percent. For strength speed the band tension must be greater than the weight on the barbell. Example, two strong lifters at Westside made a single lift with 700 pounds band tension plus 600 pounds of barbell weight on a parallel box. The ideal amount of lifts for strength speed is seven lifts. This is recommended by A.S. Prilepin's work published in 1974.

There are sports scientists who find no advantage in accommodating resistance. The author believes this happened due to the machines that were used. They offered much different bar speeds during concentric and eccentric phases. The machines were used mostly for rehab and held no advantage over free weight exercises. But the author has had great success with using a combination of free weight and band tension. Now the barbell makes it possible to develop motion while the bands added to the bar causes accommodating resistance. Bands do not control the movement pattern of the barbell, the lifter does that.

Other Methods, Accentuation

The accentuation method is designed to train strength in only the range of the sport movement where high force is maximal. It causes major muscle activity at the extreme points near both ends of the range of motion. Here are a few examples:

- Reverse hypers: The movement allows the athlete to maximize the work of the lower back, glutes and hamstrings.

- Tricep extension: Here one places almost the entire work on the tricep muscles by doing the arm extension with little or no lat movement.

- Back extension: Also isolates small portion of the back.

Peak-Contraction Principle

The peak-contraction method attempts to build strength in the weakest position. This is a sticking point, or scientists refer to it as a mini max, meaning the minimal amount of effort can be applied at the point of maximum resistance.

CHAPTER 10

Conjugate System of Training

The conjugate system of training was first introduced to an experimental group of 70 highly skilled athletes and weightlifters at the famed Dynamo Club in 1972 by Verkhoshansky and other Soviet sports scientists by using a group of 20 to 45 special and classical exercises.

After the experiment only one lifter was satisfied and the others wanted more exercises. Dr. Medvedev selected at least 100 programs for the coach to rotate from as he found fit for a particular athlete. Once an athlete accommodates to a set program a detraining effect will occur. This called for rotating special exercises that were close in structure to the lifts or events the athlete had chosen. Switching the training program causes a contrast that furthers the functional state of the body although many think the rotation of special exercise is only the end of the conjugate concept. However, the author has started 14-year-old boys completely in the Westside system. The word "completely" in this context means that we used special exercises to perfect form by bringing up the weakest muscle groups and to bring forth the advantages of their strongest muscle groups.

The conjugate concept is not limited to just exercises at Westside, but the loading in volumes and intensity zone for their periodization. Accommodation can also occur when the same volume or intensity is constantly used. The wave periodization Westside uses for speed strength ranges from 75 percent to 85 percent in a three week pendulum wave. With the next wave as it swings back to 75 percent, the athlete also uses a different bar or changes the type of accommodating resistance.

Each week on M-E days for any lift a new special exercise is trained. This illustrates a fatal mistake many make by doing the same exercise at 90 percent or more for three weeks in a row. For changing volume to avoid accommodation a new set of small special exercises are chosen that work the very same muscle groups but in a slightly different way. This applies for jumping exercises or the time it takes to run a predetermined distance by using some amount of resistance. A small change can be the width of a pressing grip or the stance while squatting or jumping. Even shoes can change things greatly with a high heel or no heel. We all know how a diet can change your body or a restoration method. And lastly, reading the author's views on the Conjugate System can possibly change how you think about special means.

CHAPTER 11

Speed Strength

Speed strength is the ability to exert maximal force during high speed movement. This special strength is trained at intermediate velocity roughly .8 to .9 m/s.

According to data from weight lifting of the highest ranks, 50 percent of the lifts are trained at 75 percent to 85 percent of a one rep max. This data was determined from 780 cases. Weightlifting is a speed strength sport, thus A.D. Ermakov and N.S. Atanasov show the distribution of loads ranging from 75 percent to 85 percent proves this. However, weightlifting is a strength speed sport first and a speed strength sport second with weights at 90 percent and above representing about 20 percent of all training while barely 20 percent of all lifts are at 70 percent and lower.

The Westside periodization model shows the same percents are used for speed strength for a powerlifter or by using the combination of resistance methods made popular by the author. Westside training uses barbell weight plus rubber bands or chains or both to accommodate resistance as well as provide an overspeed eccentrics effect.

Regardless of the exercise, the five classical lifts trained at 75 percent to 85 percent will develop speed strength. A curl trained at the 75 percent to 85 percent range also will build speed strength. Speed strength can produce speed in overcoming small loads and is needed if one's goal is to overcome large resistance rapidly due to high muscle tension.

Maximal mechanical power (Pmm) can be achieved when force and velocity are about one-third of maximum speed or about .8 m/s. This is done best with the combination of resistance method where in a three-week wave to the percent of a one rep max you use a range from 50 percent to 60 percent with 25 percent band tension at lockout. The bands ensure overspeed eccentrics for a greater stretch reflex in the bottom reducing barbell deceleration almost completely. This is known as The Dynamic Method.

To develop speed strength all three—speed strength, explosive speed and slow strength—must be trained in a weekly, monthly and a yearly plan. There is much involved in the success to speed strength development including the coordination of the percent muscle units that are required to do the task. Coordination depends also on the potential of the CNS. Maximal strength matters greatly, but only if the athlete is well rested.

The use of the conjugate system is of upmost importance with the special exercises because the development of speed strength is connected biomechanically close to the sporting event. It is possible to become too strong for an event if only max-effort work is performed. Why? As resistance grows velocity slows. But the Westside periodization is trained by a percent of a one rep max. This means that if your squat is 400 pounds and you train at 80 percent for speed strength the bar is loaded to 320 pounds then it should move roughly .8m/s.

On training for speed strength, working with too light of weight will not allow enough time to develop full strength, only explosive strength. This explains why when throwing in track implements the coach must choose the correct weight shot for a certain purpose. This explains why when hitting a mini max or sticking point, sometimes it requires one try two methods; one to become strongest in that area or to become much faster in the same area.

When repeating the same exercises too often a speed barrier or mini-max occurs. One must change special exercises including jumping exercises to avoid accommodation. Remember, train what you don't possess. If you are weak, do more training of speed and slow strength. If you are very strong but slow, train speed and explosive strength more.

It is common knowledge that to increase the velocity of a shot you must use two heavier shots followed by a standard one. This is the contrast method. When the body expects the effort to be the same after training with a heavier implement, then immediately throwing a lighter implement falls under the reactive method. This happens when one forces specific demands on the nervous system.

To develop speed, three methods are mostly used:

1. **Heavy-light method**. First lift a heavy barbell for one to two reps at 90 percent plus. Then reduce load by 20 percent and do three to six repetitions as powerfully and as fast as possible.

2. **Weight release method.** In the former Soviet Union one would load 80 percent of a one rep max, lower weight to chest, knee or into a squat, then with the help of two spotters unload 20 percent leaving 60 percent on the bar and explode eccentrically to lockout. To make it more convenient, Bob Kowasick made a device that hooks to the barbell. As one reaches the bottom of the lift the weight releaser upon hitting the floor will fall off the bar with the amount of weight desired, then immediately return concentrically as powerfully as possible.

3. **Static Dynamic Method.** This works by pulling, pushing or squatting on a bar that does not move, meaning static or isometrically. You build muscle tension from 80 percent to 100 percent for a few exertions then pull, push or squat with a much lighter bar, roughly 60 percent for a few reps. Three to 10 reps can be performed as long as speed does not slow down. This is referred to as the after-effect phenomenon.

COMPENSATORY ACCELERATION TRAINING OR CAT

This system calls for one to accelerate the barbell throughout the entire concentric phase to avoid barbell deceleration. (Dr. Fred Hatfield said no one can lift a heavy barbell slow, but one must exert maximum force to the barbell. With a submaximal weight, however, one can ease off near completion. Unfortunately, this is wrong according to Newton's second law $F=MA$.) CAT is, of course, known as the dynamic method. This method is connected to maximal strength, but will not build maximal strength due to the fact that it is impossible to attain Fmm in fast movements against intermediate resistance. Its main purpose is to improve the rate of force development and explosive strength. CAT is for medicine ball throws, jumping for max height or lifting a submaximal weight. Always try to attain the highest possible speed with a submaximal effort.

CHAPTER 12

Static Dynamic Development

Dr. A Bondarchuk, an expert of track and field events, would use the static dynamic method extensively for his track athletes. It was done by exerting force roughly from 80 percent to 100 percent muscle tension for a few reps or exertions, then going to a barbell preloaded to 70 percent and doing very explosive lifts for speed-strength development with great success. Also, using the same method of static dynamic work was Y.V. Verkhoshansky. He also found great success for his athletes for track and field and weightlifting. These giants of the sports science world found it was the greatest method of raising explosive strength. Relaxed overcome by a dynamic effort also is one of the best methods done together. This is also called the catch and release method.

Many special exercises were developed for throwing events. One such exercise was throwing hammers for the javelin and another was throwing clubs. The East Germans made a competition for boys and girls. Of course, the shot putter must rely on max strength due to the weight of a shot. While a javelin thrower must rely on explosive strength and speed.

This is shown by research on the release of both implements. The shot release is measured at close to 14m/s while a javelin release can be above 30m/s. While a shot weighs 60 pounds and a javelin weighs 0.8 pounds. So understand what you are trying to accomplish with your athletes. Much more can be learned by reading *Track and Field* and also *Track and Field: The East German Textbook of Athletics* both by Gerhardt Schmolinsky.

Speed for running can be developed for sprint speed endurance by doing the interval type training for sprinting for 100 meters, 200 meters, 300 meters and 400 meters for a set amount of repetitions depending on the level of preparedness.

By doing short distance runs you will increase not only maximum speed, but also acceleration plus sprinting endurance. Other common methods are downhill and uphill sprints, high speed runs from a crouch start or standing start, and runs in a harness up to 80 percent to 120 meters. There is also powerwalking with a weight sled loaded to bodyweight for 60 meters to 200 meters and powerwalking for 400 meters for speed endurance. You can sprint with a weight sled loaded with 20 kilograms for men and 10 kilograms for women. If you push a wheelbarrow at high speed it increases stability and balance. You can start acceleration at middle or final stages of 80 meter to 150 meter walking. Then there is running in place in a belt squat machine where you attach a belt to the waist with weight hanging between legs by a cable hooked to a weight stack. This method builds unheard of strength endurance in the running muscles for any length of race.

Power walking with a weight sled should be included in any running program as much as possible. After learning how to run in all stages of a race, strength and power must be raised as high as the athlete's capability. There is an epidemic in track from high school to the pro level in the form of not only shin splints, but also hairline fractures of the lower legs. This should never occur. The coach was most likely once a runner and they had shin splints or the same hairline fractures their athletes are enduring today. This is inexcusable. Has the coach not found a better way? Does he not remember the physical pain that came with this nagging injury? But, even more damaging is the physical pain by not performing at their best.

There have been studies that confirm that less running and more explosive weight training increases running performance. One such study entitled (what?) showed explosive strength training improves five-kilometer running time by improving economy and muscle power. Not only did their running time increase, but more importantly, the running workout time was reduced by 32 percent. More can be found in Barry Ross' book *Underground Secrets to Faster Running*. Sprinters can produce five times bodyweight on each step. This is tremendous stress on the body, but many are capable of this force. But no sprinter is capable of lifting five times their bodyweight or even able to approach five times bodyweight of force production using a submaximal weight with maximal speed.

I have heard old men are set in their ways but I have found that young men are set in their ways too then they turn into old men. Don't be that man. Instead, look for a better and safer way to train your athletes. It's your responsibility to the athlete and their sporting career.

The jumping and weight training program in this book will be of great value to anyone's running career. Westside is known for its legendary absolute strength feats, but our explosive strength feats are spectacular as well. Just consider for example the 50.2-inch box jump by a 17-year-old high school girl and the 63.5-inch box jump by an intern doing studies at Westside.

PROVEN METHODS OF STRENGTH DEVELOPMENT

MAXIMAL EFFORT METHOD

The Maximal Effort Method involves lifting the most weight on a training day, which is made possible by level of preparedness.

The volume must be kept minimal, while aiming for the most weight possible for one rep. The Bulgarian's used this method constantly, but did not focus on an all-time max, instead they based it on a day-to-day system. Westside, like the Soviet's, bases max effort success on breaking an all-time record, mostly on a special barbell exercise or a jump with resistance.

This method is proven best for improving intramuscular and intermuscular coordination. It is known that the muscles, as well as the CNS, respond to the load placed on them. This method causes the highest muscle unit activation with optimal discharge frequency. It can be very taxing if the same exercise is repeated over and over again. The Westside method calls for the athlete to change a special exercise or jump each workout to avoid accommodation. It should be performed two out of seven days, one for the upper body and one for the lower body. The max effort day should be done 72 hours after a dynamic method workout for the same body parts, meaning upper body or lower body workouts. For a weightlifting style, a max effort day barbell volume is close to 60 percent of a dynamic workout. For the powerlifter, where much larger jumps are made, the volume is closer to 40 percent of a dynamic workout. Both weight workouts consist of a ratio of 20 percent barbell lifts and 80 percent special exercises that are constant small special exercises for a lacking muscle group.

In training, one can become excited, but should avoid high emotional stress. This should instead be saved for the contest. Work up to one rep, trying for an all-time record. This keeps bodyweight low and maximum strength at the highest level. Three and five rep maxes build strength endurance, but this is not the objective of max effort. An over 90 percent record breaking phase can be kept by a proper rotating system. Westside uses the max effort method on those 14-years-old and above, and has done so with no injury to young athletes.

DYNAMIC EFFORT METHOD

The Dynamic Effort Method is for lifting or throwing a less than maximal load at the highest possible speed. F=MA

For explosive strength, use weights at 30 to 40 percent. This is high velocity training. For speed strength, use weights at 75 to 85 percent in intermediate velocity. For explosive power, the reps can be up to ten reps without the movement velocity slowing down. For speed strength, the reps should not exceed six reps. With a dynamic workout, the sets are repeated at a set weight each week for a predetermined percentage. Use a three-week pendulum wave at 75 percent, 80 percent and 85 percent. Then roll back to 75 percent and repeat a second three-week pendulum wave. This is done throughout the year for either explosive or speed strength development.

Use Compensatory Acceleration Training: push or pull as fast, and with as much force, as possible throughout the entire range of motions due to bar deceleration. A much more effective method is a combination of different resistance methods the author made popular. This calls for attaching chains or rubber bands to the bar to accommodate resistance. Bands are superior to chains for overspeed eccentrics. This method is a vital part of the programming. It is not used for maximal strength because of the existence of the explosive-strength deficit, but as your maximal strength grows and the top weight becomes lower, it is of most importance to move so its maximal weights of a certain percentage at a constant speed of an IRM. This means that 80 percent of 420 pounds or 320 pounds would move at the same speed as 80 percent of 800 pounds or 640 pounds. For programming, it is important to train all three velocities in a weekly plan that evolves into a monthly plan, then a yearly plan, and eventually a multi-year plan.

REPEATED EFFORT METHOD

The Repeated Effort Method calls for lifting a non-maximal load until near failure.

Only the final repetitions are responsible for building maximal force possible in a fatigued state. More information on all three scientifically proven methods of strength training can be found in *The Science and Practice of Strength Training, Second Edition* by V.M. Zatsiorsky.

This method builds hypertrophy where it is needed. At Westside the Repeated Effort Method is not used on the five classical lifts. It can be dangerous due to the fact that some muscle groups are stronger than others. If you have strong legs, but a weak lower back, you may suffer a lower back injury by doing so. It is best to use small special exercises to address a weakness and correct muscle imbalances. For leg development, use a glute-ham developer (GHD) machine, standing leg curl machine, or inverse curl machine. You may also do leg curls with ankle weights for 200 reps per workout. For low back development, use back raises, reverse hypers, and light high-rep Goodmornings. These are just two examples of the safest and most productive methods to build muscle mass and add great volume into the program where necessary. It does no good to be strong in the wrong exercises.

Now we have discussed all three proven methods for strength training. How are these organized into a weekly plan?

THE PLAN

Friday is the day for speed or explosive strength squats and pulls. Saturday is the day for speed or explosive strength pressing of all styles. Wednesday is max effort pressing of all styles. There are 72 hours between squats and pulls for recovery. The barbell lifts consist of only 20 percent of the total volume and small special exercises make up 80 percent. The rest intervals are 60 seconds for speed or explosive strength days. For max effort work, the rest intervals should be two to three minutes. This ensures a very dense training session. Use short rest intervals for small special exercises, including jumping. When races are scheduled for the weekend, use a max effort press to stimulate the CNS.

It is advisable to do two workouts in one day. The evening workout can be jumping or power sled work. A third option is to select a small special exercise and go with short 45-second rest intervals. For example, standing leg curls plus glute-ham raises. For upper body, chin-ups or rows with either a barbell or dumbbells. Choose the exercise wisely and be sure to rotate them for accommodation, when necessary.

To adapt to training is to never fully adapt. Take one day at a time and the system will be very simple to understand. Do an eyeball test on yourself, if needed, to see what muscle group is subpar. That is the muscle group that needs special attention. See the periodization chapter for circulations.

This system was perfected by the former Soviet Union sports scientists As they used the highest skilled athletes along with their top sports scientists to create the greatest special strength methods to date. By using this system, based on top weight lifters and track and field athletes, Westside Barbell has developed the strongest powerlifting gym of all-time. There are two ways to train, the right way, and the wrong way. No matter the sport, the Westside way is the right way, as scientifically proven.

Reduce Running and Add the Right Strength Training

You must look at your track career. Is it a short trip to high school then you are done? Or, is it a long journey aimed towards the Olympics or a world championship? This view can take anyone, twelve-years-old and up, to the highest level. It takes talent, drive, a top coach, and special equipment. If your goal is to out-run the nine-year-old girl next door, then a pair of Red Ball Jets and a gym track will do. But, if you strive to be the greatest, you must include special training on special equipment to get to the top.

EXPLOSIVE-STRENGTH TRAINING

There are far too many injuries in track events due to too much running, improper use of depth jumps, and Olympic-style weight lifting movements. No single weightlifting—meaning the clean and snatch—will build explosive power by itself. Any barbell lift will build explosive strength if trained at 30 percent of a one rep max. It will be at a fast velocity where explosive strength is built. The real answer is related to the highest muscle recruitment. And that doesn't mean the weight lifting clean or snatch, which will only improve the clean and snatch, but rather on sport-related muscle recruitment patterns. A better option, according to a study by Leena Paavolainen, is reducing running by 32 percent and replacing it with explosive-strength training. The author suggests reducing sprinting by at least 50 percent and instead including a very sophisticated program that was made possible by more than 40 years of experience.

There is a constant battle between a coach's approach to training and a scientific viewpoint. If you want to move faster, you must lift heavy weights. No one can lift a heavy weight slow, but rather one tries to lift it as fast as possible. This produces high force. (See "Hill Equation of Muscle Contraction" in *Supertraining* 2003, Sixth Edition.) To improve sprint times, you must gain strength with minimal or no weight gain. This program works for each velocity of special strength training. This means following the precise intensities and volume discussed in the chapter on periodization. It is well thought out and proven to be the most effective method. Pick the correct small special exercises to include, and take a large part of the running portion out of your programming.

BELT SQUAT MACHINE

Westside has a specially designed belt squat machine. It has an attachment that goes around the athlete's waist, as a way to traction the spine, while performing a style of walking or standing in place. Both styles build great strength in the entire lower body without pounding on the joints. The Belt Squat Machine is unparalleled in building great strength, but allows the athlete to recover quickly due to eliminating the compressing of the spine. Massive weights can be used for set time intervals. Belt squatting on boxes or free style is made easy and very productive. While belt squatting, the athlete can carry a medicine ball, or do power cleans with a Kettlebell or barbell. Even pressing or jerking weights overhead may be implemented on the machine.

HAMSTRING WORK

GHDs—A Glute-Ham Developer is a must to stimulate the entire hamstring for running or jumping or even pulling or squatting.

Inverse Hamstring Curl—This is an assisted GHD that makes it possible for anyone to use with perfect form, by adding weight making a full extension of the hamstrings possible. As one becomes stronger, reduce the weight on the lever to make the exercise harder until the athlete can do an unassisted Russian Glute-Ham Raise, which is much more effective than a GHD.

Standing Hamstring Curl—The standing hamstring curl almost duplicates the motion of running leg cycles. By combining the standing leg curl with one of the earlier mentioned devices, the hamstrings are developed completely.

Reverse Hyper™—This device will not only develop the hamstrings, but also the lower back and Gluteus Maximus. A weak lower back leads to weak hamstrings, which leads to hamstring pulls. Many times the missing link for hamstring development is the glutes. The Reverse Hyper is the key to glute development, along with static holds in the belt squat machine. Use the devices mentioned to ensure zero injuries when squatting and pulling and of course sprinting or any style of running.

HAMSTRING MAINTENANCE

Doing 200 leg curls with ankle weights of five to 20 pounds a day will ensure healthy hamstrings by building greater thickness of the sole tissue of the hamstrings. This is where the elastic energy is stored that relates to adding kinetic energy.

PLYOMETRIC SWING

Explosive strength is a must for sprinting. With the Plyometric Swing one can develop explosive strength fast and safe. The swing takes advantage of kinetic energy. Have the athlete first push themselves away from the foot plate, then as he or she swings back onto the foot plate actively stopping it, then pushing off again as fast as possible. The author has a plyometric swing with band attachments. Hooking rubber bands to it causes an overspeed eccentrics phase, raising kinetic energy for a more reversible strength. A combination of weight and band tension works best. This is best for transforming the amortization phase into elastic energy, which is then used in the concentric phase. The elastic energy is equal to the kinetic energy of the swing holding the athlete as it contacts the foot plate. Kinetic energy = mgH; where m equals mass, g equals acceleration due to gravity, and H equals the height of the swing fall. More on this can be found in *Supertraining*, Sixth Edition 2003. Remember that more velocity is better than more mass. This is just another way of building running speed without the pounding of running.

NON-MOTORIZED TREADMILL

Running on a surface that moves is much different than running on a track that does not move. A much better method is a treadmill that the athlete must actively move each time the athlete takes a step. The Westside version has band attachments to hold onto the hips, waist, or ankles. Ankle weights or a weight vest may also be used. One can walk or run on the mill, also called slat mills, much like many dog trainers use. This device can be responsible for less running as well.

STATIC DYNAMIC DEVELOPER

The author has many patents, but the Static Dynamic line is unparalleled for explosive strength development. Two great sportsmen, A. Bondarchuk and Verkhoshansky, used two proven methods for explosive strength.

1. The heavy-light method. Here, one would do one to two reps with a weight over 90 percent then immediately go to a weight of 30 percent for a set amount of reps of very explosive lifts.

2. In the second method, one would push or pull against a static bar, meaning isometrics, then move to a bar loaded at 30 percent for a set amount of reps.

The author has made a device that holds the bar static by air pressure, then as the athlete pulls, pushes, or squats against the bar, for a predetermined time, it is released and the athlete explodes through what range of motion the coach desires. The static dynamic method is the greatest method to build not only explosive strength, but also absolute strength.

The athlete has the option of using a Jones Machine that can duplicate any barbell exercise, a Plyometric Swing for jumping with several stances, and a Belt Squat Machine that can hold a static hold in either vertical or horizontal. For throwing events, a machine for throwing and kicking with a static hold overcome dynamically. You may not be able to have a static dynamic device, but the machines mentioned early in this section must be used to reach the highest sport level and prolong a career.

MORE EQUIPMENT

BARS

Safety Squat Bar

14-inch Chamber Bar

Bow Bar

Manta Ray

Front Squat Harness

SLEDS

Two Olympic 400-meter gold medalists, both seventeen-year-old girls, were trained with adding the above special devices and bars. One had a box jump of 50½ inches. The second athlete decreased her 60-meter time from 7.80 to 7.24 in just six months with no injuries. She rotated resistance, distance, special exercises, the special devices and sled work while reducing running time 40 percent.

One constantly must add new stimulus to the program to continuously break records. This is why the author suggests more correct weight training and constantly rotating weekly routines. Let's talk about the speed barrier.

THE SPEED BARRIER

If one uses the same program over and over with the same times and other characteristics, the athlete will learn only to run at the same speed.

This is known as the speed barrier. Reaction time may improve, or even strength and flexibility, but still no increase in time will take place. The answer is to stop some of the running and bring in special means to the program. This is why special devices and resistance—meaning sled pulling—must be entered into the athletes programming.

The speed barrier is very common for football players. They constantly slow down from their high school combine times to their NFL combine times. This is due to a coach having no imagination or experience. They simply do the same thing over and over, which is a form of accommodation. A sprinter can run on a track that is inclined three degrees or run behind a rabbit. He or she can sprint with a light sled (10 kilograms for women and 20 kilograms for men). No one ever thinks like the following:

> If a boy could run at 12 mph the first time he ran, how did he do it?

He did it through other activities like playground time. And maturity. Most will never run 24 mph if only running is continued. Better running form can be increased by building stronger muscle groups. By not doing the same running, one may lose the memory of time links. Characteristics of the speed barrier may be forgotten leading one to again make progress. This is why much of the running must be removed and resistance and jumping is added.

When using strength exercises it is important to remember the objective is not becoming a weight lifter, but a faster sprinter. All styles of barbell exercises must be included into the program. But, remember the exercises must increase strength in the running muscles. This is why the special exercise machines the author suggests will build the precise muscles that run. It is important to know that increasing maximal strength improves speed of movements. This is why men can run faster than women—they are stronger; end of story. But they must be trained with a weekly plan together with 72 hours separating large workouts.

An example of correct strength training can be seen below.

A 400-pound squatter will use a three-week pendulum wave with the percentages of 50, 55, and 60; with a 25 percent band tension at the top of the lift.

The sets are the same, the reps are the same and the rest intervals are the same. And most importantly so is the bar speed, $8^m/_s$. It is wrong to judge top strength and max running speed or even the shot put that way. It should be judged by who is fastest with speed strength percentages of 75 percent to 85 percent. Remember: the results of a faulty test are worthless. There are many factors to consider. One, reaction must be always improved. Ben Johnson had such a fast reaction time that they had to adjust the racing clock. Jumping and bounding improves reaction time. Special resistance training can improve endurance of all kinds. Improving jumping ability and short sprints will improve general speed. Also team sports can improve speed. To improve speed best, do not train when fatigued, or when the CNS is overstressed. It is best to do a heavy strength or speed strength workout in the morning and the explosive strength workouts in the afternoon. Explosive strength should be trained often, but in short time periods. This means box jumps, depth jumps, or bounding workouts should be concluded in a short time as to not interfere with the CNS. A reduction in speed can happen if the athlete doesn't do strength or speed work for 14 days, which underscores the need for the athlete to have a sound foundation of GPP and strength training to withstand the great demands on the body.

CHAPTER 13

PULLING EXERCISES

Advanced Weight Training

The author once wrote an article about how to increase speed for the 100 meter, but was denied publication because the matter of information was not the right protocol by the NSCA, and because I did not have a college degree or a list of references. It wasn't enough that working with me had reduced the time of a 60-meter Big Ten champ from 10.47 to 10.17 in nine weeks, and this was after the Ohio State track coach said he could not run any faster.

Training methods must come from elite athletes and filter down to the lesser athletes. Articles and studies help in this effort, but they should be based on conduct of experienced athletes. I find it problematic when a professor has a student or students tackle a subject they may not have sound experience with like the effects of a deadlift on the vertical jump in novices. Such a study was conducted by Thompson, Stock, Shields, Luera, Munayer, Mota, Carrillo, and Olinghouse. The study took 54 college-aged men and women who were familiar with any form of controlled physical activity. The deadlifts were performed in the conventional style, which refers to hands outside of the legs. A major flaw of the study was having the athletes <u>not</u> move the bar explosively. Five sets of five reps were performed. Even with this inexperience, the results were positive, meaning all produced an increase in the vertical jump. Although the participants were mostly untrained and the instructions were not perfect, the author hails their efforts in doing such research. The title of this work is *Barbell Deadlift Training Increases the Rate of Torque Development and Vertical Jump Performance in Novices.*

This brings to mind the efforts by Barry Ross to increase the running speeds of sprinters. One learns in Ross's book, *Underground Secrets to Faster Running,* that the phenomenal Allyson Felix came to Ross for weight training as a freshman. She had just been tested in a number of situations to help her performance. She tested very high in all elite levels except for one: Strength. She needed to produce and generate more force to the ground.

He knew through biomechanical studies that 90 percent of the effort to run down a track is to overcome gravity, meaning it is the vertical forces that must be improved. Therefore, the weight training must be two methods mixed during the week. First, the max effort method should be used, where the largest weight possible for one rep is lifted in a slow velocity. Then, 72 hours later, the dynamic method should be used, where a submaximal weight is lifted as fast as possible due to F=MA being the objective. He had her use two velocities: 1) fast for explosive strength and 2) 30 to 40 percent of a one rep max, or 75 to 85 percent with bar weight only, or a combination of band tension and bar weight, at intermittent velocity for speed strength. Mr. Ross used the deadlift to increase Allyson's power. It did not cause an increase in bodyweight, as that would not help, but rather hurt the power to weight ratio.

At Westside, we believe the deadlift is most critical to explosive power. Here is the story of an 18-year-old female sprinter. After working with us during her high school years, she left Westside in the fall of 2014 to go to college. She left at age 17 with a 50½-inch box jump. She returned to Westside after the end of a bad track season in which her times slowed down. Her coach had told her that her muscle and tendon elasticity was low. Yet the coach did not have her perform any box jumps throughout the whole season. This led to her returning to Westside with a 42-inch box jump max. The first three-week pendulum wave led her to produce a 53½-inch box jump record as of July 10, 2015.

Mr. Barry Ross is very well versed in the world of elite sprinting and has a very high IQ in weight training. He wrote a simple book, consisting of 86 pages, packed with some of the most comprehensive information that any coach could utilize to their athletes benefit.

Westside Barbell is the most accomplished special strength gym in the world. We have seven women with an over 500-pound deadlift, 22 men over 800 pounds, and two over 900 pounds. On the other end of maximal strength is explosive strength. Explosive strength is the ability to rapidly increase force (Tidow, 1990). Jumping ability is an action of explosive strength in the form of a jump. As of July 10, 2015, the women's box jump record is 53½-inch and the men's is 63½-inch. The author is only stating these facts as a way to validate the training method you find in this book.

Two days are used in a weekly plan. First is the max effort, or ME, day. This may also be described as shock methods. Many know the shock method only as muscle stimulation by means of absorbing the KE of a fall, but it is really any ME attempt to maximally stimulate the muscular system and central nervous system. *Supertraining* lists several shock methods on page 283 of the 2003 Sixth Edition. Here is just a small list of Westside ME methods:

Rack Pull	High Box Squat
Box Pull	Low Box Squat
Power Clean	Contrast Methods
Power Snatch	Maximal Eccentrics
Goodmorning	Concentric Squats

This method is used to develop maximal strength, which means doing something one has never done before. Each week, a new barbell lift is rotated into the plan. Most often, three lifts for one single rep is performed. After warming up, perform one rep at about 90 percent of your one rep max, one closer to a previous one rep max, and then a small new record. Example for a 500-pound deadlift: 455x1, 485x1, and finally 505x1 for a personal record. Then, move to small special exercises. They should make up to 80 percent of the total volume. Only 20 percent with the barbell, meaning a squat, press, or pull. You must understand that a squat or Goodmorning will contribute to raising your deadlift. The more exercises, in terms of those with a barbell, the greater one's chance of success by eliminating effects of the law of accommodation. For the sprinter, the amount of force that one can deliver to the ground depends partly on technique, but mostly on how strong your muscles are. This is why ME, or shock methods, must be utilized weekly. It must be noted that distance runners can also benefit from strength training as well. It is proven in a study published by Leena Paavolainen in 1999, titled "Explosive-Strength Training Improves 5-km Running Time by Improving Running Economy and Muscle Power." It is referred to in *Underground Secrets to Faster Running* by Barry Ross. They cut their running time by 32 percent, with very positive results.

We now introduce the second day for explosive and speed strength development. It is referred to as Dynamic Effort. The DE method is not used for increasing maximal strength, but only to improve the rate of force development and explosive strength. It is one thing to be stronger, while it is quite another to display it. When training for explosive strength, the weights should range from 30 to 40 percent bar weight, plus 25 percent band tension. The reps can be up to ten reps if the bar velocity does not slow down. The total lifts can be 60 max per workout. It is best done with a combination of bar weight, plus 25 percent band tension at lockout, but with tension at the bottom of the lift. The rubber bands play two roles. One is AC, accommodating resistance. AC will eliminate bar deceleration, causing maximal tension throughout the entire range of motion. Secondly, it causes an overspeed eccentric effect, for greater reversible strength. This causes greater KE by increasing bar velocity. To increase KE, it is better to increase velocity than mass. The rubber bands work much like muscles and tendons, they stretch and contract. A faster eccentric phase causes a greater force with minimal ground contact while running.

Deadlifting for Explosive Power

We have talked about ME training where the weights are maximal and the bar velocity is slow to very slow. This is where maximal force development is trained: the dynamic effort workout for rate force development (RFD).

A fast rate of force development for explosive is training at 30 to 40 percent in a three-week pendulum wave. The reps can be six to 10, as long as the bar speed does not slow down. The style is sumo style, in which the feet are much wider than the hips. This style puts much emphasis on the lower body muscles used in running such as the hips, hamstrings, and adductors, and less emphasis on the lower back, to lessen the chance of injury. To sumo pull, one must pull the hips to the bar and down as low as possible, while pushing the feet, which are turned outward, somewhat as the bar breaks from the floor, allowing the pelvic to come forward as the shoulders are going backwards. Again, this isolates the lower body running muscles. After completing the first rep, completely lower the bar, as fast as possible, and touch and go the remainder of the reps in a set. For an explosive response, the eccentric must be fast to build a strong stretch-reflex.

Always use the combinations of methods training, meaning adding 25 percent of your one rep max to the bar plus the 30 to 35 and 40 percent in a three-week wave. The fast eccentric phase will not add muscle mass but great reversal strength. One must use minimal ground contact, just as if you are running. The sumo deadlift will build great lateral strength. Like it or not, all great sprinters will push out to the sides in the very beginning, gaining block clearance. Usain Bolt is criticized for almost moving outside of his lane at the beginning of the race. Perhaps he has highly built up the hip muscles that are built during the sumo lift. Remember, use a fast eccentric phase and barely touch the platform, then explode concentrically to lockout. If you are an explosive athlete in an explosive event, YOU MUST TRAIN EXPLOSIVELY. Read the periodization chapter for total sets and reps with the optimal number of lifts. Many use only two velocities for track: slow with weights over 90 percent for two to three reps per set for two to three sets, then 30 to 40 percent weights as a contrast for explosive strength.

Westside, however, uses a third velocity—intermediate—for speed strength. The barbell will move at approximately $8^m/_s$. This training teaches one to accelerate throughout the entire range of motion. A three-week pendulum wave is performed at 50 to 55 and 60 percent of a one rep max, plus 25 percent band tension making the lockout 75-80-85 percent of a one rep max. The bands will eliminate nearly all of your barbell deceleration as your strength curve improves at the completion of a lift. The sumo style is best for the same reasons that we use it for explosive strength training. The number of reps should range from two to five per set, and the sets can range from five to 12. The total number of lifts should be about 24 or 25 per workout.

To train speed strength for athletes, use a fast eccentric phase. After completing the first rep, employ the touch-and-go method, just as you would in explosive strength training. One may lower the barbell plates onto rubber mats, or even foam blocks. The deadlifts may be done after squatting for explosive or speed strength. They could also be done after ME training. This will cause a contrast using the heavy and the light systems.

Finally, for the coach who uses Olympic (oly-style) lifting, follow the workout below for explosive or speed strength. If the methodology sounds familiar, it is. The author has, since 1982, followed the recommendations of A.S. Prilepin (1974). Prilepin's work was based on 1,000 top athletes from Europe, including weight lifters as well as track and field athletes. There was no research available on the powerlifts. At Westside we knew we must become much faster, so we followed the great research of the top sports scientists from the former Soviet Union. There are many special strengths; one or more of which may suffer if not trained in the same weekly plan, which of course leads to a monthly, yearly, and multi-year plan. This is stated by Zatsiorsky, but Westside has found that all can be trained simultaneously, week in week out. Zatsiorsky (1995) presents these rules in the book, *Science of Sports Training, Second Edition*, by T. Kurz.

1. The force values shown in slow movements are close to those in isometric tensions.

2. In fast concentric movements, the force value will diminish as the velocity of movement increases. (This correlates to the findings of the Hill Equation for Muscle Contraction, 1938.)

Zatsiorsky also states that there is no relationship between the force values in extremely fast movements of little to no resistance and maximal isometric tension or maximal strength. For example, take a javelin, shot put, and a barbell. The release of a javelin is about $30^{m}/_{s}$, while a shot put is $14^{m}/_{s}$ at release. And lastly, the release of a heavy barbell, while a weightlifter separates it from the platform, moves at about $6^{m}/_{s}$.

Remember MSF, mass specific force? Look for strength gains, not just larger muscles. Sometimes smaller men are stronger than larger men, due mostly to directed strength training, rather than just hypertrophy. Strength must produce adaptations of the nervous system in terms of learning and coordination as well as muscle hypertrophy, but not like bodybuilders with high reps near, or even to, failure. Most machines with which muscle is built, but not motion like a weightlifter or powerlifter, force one to become more coordinated.

The strength training for explosive and speed strength was first used with Olympic lifters, like the snatch and clean, or clean and jerk. Remember, two movements build reversal strength. The hang clean, when one lowers the barbell to shin or knee level, then quickly pulls it upward, and the jerk, where the lifter re-bends the legs, then immediately thrusts the barbell overhead.

Oly-Style Workouts

Regardless of the amount of weight being lifted, you must use the same three percentages for the three-week pendulum wave. For example, the same percentages of a deadlift—say 60 percent with 25 percent band tension—will move at the same velocity as a clean or snatch with 60 percent of a one rep max with 25 percent band tension. For speed strength, you must go from snatches to deadlifts and from deadlifts to cleans. Strength can increase because of adaptation of the body's resistance training.

Adaptation will occur very quickly if the exercises stay the same. This is called accommodation, or in terms of running, the speed barrier. The Westside System constantly rotates small and large exercises. The volume with a barbell is very high to very low every 72 hours. ME is low barbell volume, plus switching between a large barbell exercise each week, for strength speed. Dynamic workouts are high volume with multiple sets each week, while raising the percentage of a one rep max each week, for three weeks straight. Then, return to week one, but change the bar or type of accommodating resistance. If the training is used over and over, year by year, it will become habitual, meaning the practicing or acting in some manner by force of habit. This constantly happens to a coach stuck in his or her own ways, not being able to look outside of the box, as they say. Saying this, one must see the scientific approach to a three-week wave, plus training for one objective, explosive, speed, or strength speed, in one workout for each, then using oly lifts and barbell jumps for explosive strength.

For the power snatch, power clean, and jump squats, the reps performed can be five. However, If and only if, the barbell speed does not suffer at additional reps above five, up to 10 reps may be done. The sets should be from five to six sets of as many as 10 reps with 30-35-40 percent in a three-week wave. Or, the sets may be 10 sets with the reps at five to six per set for those with almost all type IIB. They produce the maximal force because of their strength and speed of contraction. One may switch from the hang clean to the hang snatch every three weeks or perform the first half of the workout with one of the two, then switch and finish the workout with the other. The author prefers to switch every three weeks, as the goal is not perfecting the oly lifts, but rather increasing the rate of force development, for sprinting. The combination of resistance methods is best for sports, which means you would add rubber bands to the barbell. For jump squats, use the same method for sets and reps. Jump squats are best executed in a belt squat machine.

SPEED STRENGTH

For the snatch, clean, or clean and jerk, the sets are 5-10-12 and the reps two to five. The total lifts will be 24 to 25 per workout. For example, five sets of five reps or 12 sets of two reps. The average bar speed is roughly $18 ^m/_s$. Remember, one must always raise absolute strength. It is an advantage to be stronger for building explosive or speed strength. If one athlete can squat 400 pounds, their 60 percent would be 240 pounds. If another athlete can squat 500 pounds., their 60 percent would be 300 pounds. The key to success is that the 300 pounds, or 60 percent of a 500-pound max, moves at the same speed as the 400-pound squat at 60 percent, or 240 pounds.

For sprinting, and even much longer distances, greater ground force is crucial to faster running times while maintaining minimal ground contact. This was proven by a Leena Paavolainen study of 1999 for five-kilometer runs with added explosive strength training and reduced running by 32 percent. They also improved their times without increasing Vo2 max, much like sprinting greater ground force by adding more muscle power decreases ground contact in distance running. Paavolainen's study proved that a 5k runner with an average stride of two meters would use 2,500 strides to complete the race. It also showed that an $1/100^{th}$ of a second reduction in ground contact would reduce their time by 25 seconds. This can be found in *Underground Secrets to Faster Running* by Barry Ross (2005). It is advisable to do a weight program of maximal effort, meaning one rep, the morning of a race to increase the stimulation of the CNS. To close, the "experts" say that one special strength does not carry over to another special strength. However, the author has found and proven that they can influence each other when trained in the same week, week after week, leading to a monthly, yearly, and multi-yearly plan.

There are three methods of eliciting maximum muscle tension.

1. **The Maximal Effort Method**: Overcoming maximum resistance that causes maximal muscle tension. This is done for advancing speed strength sports.

2. **The Repetition Method to Failure**: Using less than a maximum load for reps until failure. When using light weights, only the very last reps will benefit strength gains. This method is used mostly with small special exercises

3. **The Dynamic Effort Method**: Lifting a submaximal weight at maximal speed. For sports, it is used for the development of speed strength and explosive strength.

While training, do not become emotionally stimulated or psyched up. Save that for the competition.

CHAPTER 14

SPECIAL SURFACE JUMPING

One must get the most out of training. Do not let training get the most out of you. Like all else, power training jumps must be rotated, as well as the surface on which they are performed. Most jumping, as well as landing, is done on rubber or wood gym floors. However, other alternatives must be introduced to the athletes training in order to increase explosive strength and direct jumping ability. Records must be kept on the height of the jumps off gym mats, foam, and sand. Jumping and landing on soft surfaces will absorb some of the downward energy as it takes away the advantages of the stretch, shorten cycle. It also makes training much easier on the joints, while causing the muscles to work extra hard, improving your box or vertical jump.

It is impossible for one to jump off a soft surface as high as one can jump from a hard surface because the athlete's muscles must work much harder with a soft surface. But, when going back to a hard surface, or sporting event, one will be able to jump much higher. Westside has not only jumped off of a foam surface, but also performed the squat and deadlift, with great results. It was performed by the top 10 ranked lifters only, but no statistics on the actual lifts were recorded. One subject was the lifter with the greatest coefficient squat ever of 1,210 pounds at a bodyweight of 271. A study entitled, "The Effects of Sand Training on Jumping Abilities of Junior Volleyball Players," by Rajkumar Sharma and Devarishi Kumar Chaubey, showed positive results of improved explosive leg strength when jumping in the sand vertically and horizontally, and then jumping in grass.

THE METHOD

The squat and deadlift training was done for a development of speed strength. Using bar weight ranging from 50 to 60 percent and an additional 25 percent band tension at the top, 20 lifts per workout are performed for the squat and 12 for the deadlift. The deadlifting is done sumo style as a way to get total body strength training in, especially for the glutes, hips, and hamstrings. Plus, the calves must then work extra hard to stabilize the lifter's center of mass.

All methods of jumping were performed for two workouts per week, Monday and Friday. An example would be jumping with a Kettlebell, weight vest, barbells, ankle weights, and a combination of two or three of these resistances. Running can be extremely taxing on the athlete due to constant pounding on the ground with ones bodyweight, plus the added resistance of the force of gravity. The best results were from depth jumps followed by a jump, as high as possible, from at least a two meter drop into sand, for improving muscle strength in the legs (Dursenv and Raevsky, 1978). This could be done when dropping into eight-inch foam blocks, from two meters or higher. This would be impossible when landing on a hard surface, due to the high risk of injury involved. Often when doing depth drops at one meter or higher, the purpose is building absolute strength, not explosive strength because of the much longer amortization phase. When landing in foam or sand, the amortization phase is much slower because much of the force from the fall is absorbed by the soft landing, placing most of the stress on the muscles rather than joints. Standing in foam or sand, or landing in foam or sand, can build great strength in the legs. A second method at Westside calls for the athlete to not only stand on foam blocks, but also sit onto a box with a foam block. The hips, upper legs, and glutes cause a much greater amount of muscle mass to be absorbed, which eliminates much of the plyometric advantages of the stretch reflex. This style of depth jumping can and should be used during in-season training, as well as off-season.

A 20-year-old powerlifter at Westside Barbell, Mike Brown, had gone from 700 pounds to 725 pounds in the deadlift during his last six months of training. After doing his speed deadlifts while standing on foam blocks, and doing his speed strength squatting not only standing on foam blocks, but also sitting on an eight-inch thick foam block, for the next six months, his best deadlift of 725 pounds went straight up to 804 pounds. This was mainly due to doing both of these 20 speed strength squats and 12 speed strength deadlifts per week.

A pro football player, weighing 237 pounds at 6'1", came to Westside with a 4.62-second 40-yard run, a 48-inch box jump, and a combined vertical jump of 38 inches. Training at Westside for three months, then to another pro combine, his 40 yards dropped to 4.42, and his vertical jump increased to 44 inches. The box jump also increased from 48 inches to 60 inches. Much of the jumping workouts were performed on foam blocks, as well as sitting onto a box with an eight-inch foam block on top while jumping onto a second box.

A third experiment conducted at Westside was done with a third-year NFL lineman, Pete Champion, from the Raiders. By sitting on a 17-inch bench, in the box squat style, and doing a long jump, Pete made the longest standing long jump of his career in just one weekend at Westside.

This is a long-proven method that not only has produced the largest two squats, 1,267 and Donny Thompson's 1,265, but also has produced the two greatest ever male coefficient squats, 1,180 pounds at a bodyweight of 264 pounds and Dave Hoff's 1,210 pounds at a bodyweight of 271. Plus, Laura Phelps Sweatt's record of a 775-pound squat at a bodyweight of 165 pounds. And to date, a 53½-inch box jump by Shalon, and a 63½-inch box jump by Joe, an intern at Westside Barbell. Joe had no previous depth jumping experience, only jumping upwards with a step to start the stretch reflex. This method is known as the momentum-impulse relationship to calculate work, force, and velocity. More on this can be found in an article written by Paula Lightsey entitled "A Formula for Measurements of Leg Power in the Vertical Jump."

For horizontal jumping, sit back and down onto a box with the shin posted parallel to the placement of the work on the glutes, hips, and, most importantly, the hamstrings. If one were to sit back to this extent, one would fall backwards to the ground, but not when following this procedure. The athlete should sit onto the box and rock backwards, swinging the arms as well, while lifting the feet off the ground. Then the athlete should swing the arms forward as he or she slams the feet back onto the floor and jumps up onto the box, or for horizontal jumping, jumps forward for height as well as distance. For best results, place an obstacle to jump over. This can be done for single or multiple jumps. Much like jumping out of sand, when jumping from gym mats or foam, much of the kinetic energy is lost upon sitting onto the box. While rocking backwards and then forwards on the box, many things occur:

1. Rocking breaks up the eccentric concentric chain, much like in running.

2. Some of the muscles are held static, overcome by a dynamic action.

3. Some of the muscles are relaxed, overcome by a dynamic action.

Two and three are the two greatest methods to develop explosive and absolute strength. Remember to use several methods for explosive power through the use of special jumping exercises.

CHAPTER 15

TIME RELATED DISTANCE WORKOUTS

Time under muscle tension can mean a variety of different things to a lot of different people. But to the author, a specific race, meaning a 60 meter that takes less than 75 seconds or a 10,000 meter that takes approximately 30 minutes, should be trained by special means for the same time, or slightly longer, than it takes to complete the race. In short sprints up to 100 meters, acceleration is the key component to race success. As the distance of the race grows, speed endurance plays a larger and more precise element of the athletes training. The longer the distance, the more work and rest intervals must be introduced into the special training measures protocol. For the longest races—20,000, 25,000, and 30,000 meters—more intervals of training and rest are added.

Many athletes just run for the majority of their training. By doing so, they become acquainted with the speed barrier. This occurs from doing too many speed exercises from a dynamic stereotype in the central nervous system. More can be found in *Science of Sports Training*, T. Kurz (2001). This can happen throughout the entire race, or for just a part of the race. It can even be the start. If one is not trained correctly and repeatedly performs the same mistakes, the start will not improve, and may actually become worse. If one cannot maintain top speed at the end of a sprint, more running will not cure the problem. The more repetition done, the stronger the so-called speed barrier becomes. The runner learns to move at a certain speed. Can this be overcome? Yes.

There are two methods used to break the speed barrier. One is to encourage the athlete to do better. This method, in the author's experience, is seldom successful for top athletes as they must be self-motivated throughout their entire career. The second method is to reduce much running so that the athlete will forget the difficulty of the race, or a certain part of the race.

Many will stop completely during the event or exercise and only perform special exercises. This is known in sports science as delayed transmutation and can be found in the book *Science and Practice of Strength Training*, by V. M. Zatsiorsky (2006). The author suggests that special means must be introduced into the program, but segments of the race must be practiced as well as the special means training. This may include changing the volume and intensity zones of the athlete. This could mean more ME work to raise maximal strength, or adding more volume to the jumping, or 30 to 40 percent weight training for explosive strength. Also, one must increase speed strength work of the 75 to 85 percent nature. Or, insert more recovery methods. Remember to train optimally, not minimally, or, the major sin of a majority of coaches, maximally. This will lead to chronic overtraining. A coach must understand that any eccentric muscle actions are performed like running, or worse running downhill. Even if not performed at top speed, it can cause muscle soreness. This can happen most often in lesser skilled or under prepared athletes. Before starting a full sprinting program, have a large base. One must raise GPP to reduce or eliminate injury to the athlete, because muscles grow at a much faster rate than the soft tissue, tendons, and ligaments. Remember, recovery is just as important as any other training methods.

The coach or athlete must choose the right sport. For sprinting, one must possess a great deal of explosive strength. Explosive strength is best tested by jumping or throwing. Jumping is a test that should be done by young boys or girls, at least by the age of 14. For pure speed, a short sprint is the best test. For upper body, perform medicine ball throws. While on the knees, throw a medicine ball forward from behind the head for distance.

For the sprinter, maximal strength must be raised throughout ones career. It can produce greater ground force along with minimal ground contact. We ran a test with non-athletes and athletes and found the amount of time to pick up a leg and put it down was very similar between the two groups. So what makes one run faster? Two things: the force that is applied onto the ground, and how long the foot remains on the ground. This explains why great strength to bodyweight ratio is key. Remember MSF, mass specific force, along with correct biomechanics is the key to faster running. Great maximal strength is a must for sprinting up to 400 meters. However, being very strong is one factor, but being able to display it is quite another. It requires one to produce explosive strength and maintain it for as long as possible. These two factors are most important at shorter distances, about 60 meters to 200 meters.

The athlete may be asked to parallel box squat two and a half times their bodyweight to produce enough strength and power to break world records. One must possess great strength to produce high ground force with minimal ground contact through special strength exercises such as box squats, deadlifts, and hang cleans, with an eccentric phase. In order to maintain that top strength, one must select a ground of special exercises that are done for the same time, or slightly longer, than the event. Speed of a movement can be increased by a method that duplicates the movement with great resistance, or light resistance. One method is sled walking with weights up to 300 pounds for time over a certain distance. Sixty meters is most often used with very heavy sled walks. It should take about 25 seconds to complete one trip. The athlete is producing maximal force from the first step to the last step. The sled should jerk on each step to ensure maximal ground force each time. This will build a strong start, as well as ability to maintain top speed for a longer time. This will help eliminate the deceleration period, which is where races are won or lost. Remember, this builds great strength in the running muscles.

For top speed training, pull a bodyweight sled for 60 meters. This sled to bodyweight combination works best for producing great force in each step. The weight on the sled may be changed depending on the walking surface being grass, blacktop, concrete, or running track. For distances up to 200 and 400 meters, pull the sled for a set time of 25 seconds for 200 meters and 60 seconds for 400 meters. Check the distance that the athlete covers in the set time frame and place a marker at that point. On each proceeding powerwalk, encourage the athlete to cover more distance in the allotted 25 or 60 seconds. This will build top speed for a longer time period, thus reducing the deceleration phase, where many races are lost.

An experiment done with a 26-year-old female, whose best 800 meter was 2.10 seconds, led to her cutting six seconds off her time in nine weeks, by powerwalking with a weight sled holding 45 pounds for 400 meters in 2.46 seconds. Nine weeks later, she covered it in 2.14 seconds and ran in 2.04 seconds by using this method two times per week. Another speed strength workout involved running with a safety squat bar loaded to 135 pounds for 400 meters, starting at 2.15 seconds and reducing her time during the nine weeks. A third optimal workout was pushing a wheel barrel for 400 meters. To avoid accommodation, these workouts, along with pushing up record lifts and box jumping higher, were the key to faster times. This athlete had had no gains in the six previous years of training.

For acceleration training, men use 45 pounds and women use 25 pounds. This is best done on grass to avoid lower leg overtraining and injuries. To increase speed, three methods must be employed. Perfecting reaction, the athlete must use exercises very similar to the techniques of the sport, and, use special exercises for strength and gaining jumping ability (Sozanski and Witczak, 1981).

The idea is not to build a sprinter into a top weightlifter or increase their flexibility to the point of being a contortionist. However, both must be increased, or at the minimum, maintained. No one can be too strong, too rich, or too smart. Just remember that you are trying to be a runner first, even though one must reduce at least 30 percent of the running. Even a chicken can run with its head cut off.

A belt squat on a soft box is key to all special strengths, while relieving spinal pressure. Very heavy weights build maximum strength. For speed endurance, perform sets of 60 reps for 60 seconds or 120 reps at one rep per second for two minutes, or 120 seconds. For the highly advanced distance runners, three to eight sets are optimal.

One must use many methods and exercises to reach their top potential. The athlete may be fast, or have great endurance in some exercises or tests, but not in all. Find the lacking ones and push them to exceed the best ones, and you will have found the secret of the Westside Conjugate System. For the novice, almost anything will improve performance in the beginning. But, as one becomes well-trained and more sport-specific, special exercises must be used and rotated constantly.

When training to run faster, only one thing should matter: time. This can mean reaction time. Reaction time is the time one takes to make the body react to a single stimulus or perform repetitions of the movement. When training for longer distance, meaning 5,000 meters, one continuous sled walk can be done for two or three trips. Even a 10,000-meter run can be done by doing one sled walk for 30 minutes. For the 5,000 meter, a 15-minute pull will work. For a 20,000 meter, sled walking should be done in intervals of 15 minutes for four to six sled walks per workout, once per week in the beginning of training. For a long race, like a marathon, the sled walking time can be much longer. Start with 30 minutes with a set rest interval. As your fitness grows, add time to the sled walking or reduce the time between working sets with the sled. As the race length grows, the weight on the sled should be reduced. One must train through fatigue to increase endurance, but not at the cost of bad technique. Mechanics must be perfected. Remember, build strength and this will build the ability to produce faster speeds regardless of the distance. Remember the study by Leena Paavolainen and its finding that increasing ground force by adding more muscle power decreases ground contact time even for distance running. Reducing ground contact by one $1,100^{th}$ of a second in a 5k race where it takes 2,500 strides to cover the distance, would reduce your time by 25 seconds.

Now, more on strength training. While one must increase maximal strength for any distance, you definitely must increase maximal strength for the shortest distances. For longer and longer distances, strength endurance becomes more and more important. One must use general endurance training to run long distances faster, just as a sprinter. Why? When using sport-specific endurance training, the athlete will become fatigued during the training and sports techniques will be distorted and therefore cause technique problems. This is precisely why Paavolainen reduced normal running and replaced it with explosive weight training. General endurance exercises such as the squat, presses, and special pulling exercises like cleans, snatches, and deadlifts that build the largest muscle groups, will increase the total development of the athlete.

The Conjugate System must be used not only for the large barbell exercises, but also the small special exercises. For example, for the lower body you can do calf-ham-glute raises, reverse hypers, standing leg curls, belt squats, special hip exercises, and so forth. By rotating the small exercises, often there will be no accommodation. The introvert will not need to rotate exercises as often as the extrovert, who will also want many more exercises. Use a three-week pendulum wave when doing any special strength training. On the fourth week, the intensity will go down roughly 10 percent to allow for some recovery and ensure a rate of adaptation. This can mean doing 60 belt squats in 60 seconds with 45 pounds on week one, 55 pounds on week two, and 65 pounds on week three. On the fourth week, one may switch to running with a safety squat bar for a three-week pendulum wave, starting with 135 pounds on week one, 145 pounds on week two, and finally 155 pounds on week three. One may go to a different three-week wave, such as sprinting with a wheel barrel, or go back to the belt squat and do 60 reps per minute, for three to five sets, with a rest interval of four to five minutes between sets. All workouts are followed by three or four small special exercises. When using directed endurance training, one must make the workout close in effort to the event or events that one competes in. For sprinting, do not overtax the CNS. Everyone does not recover at the same rate. This can be due to lack of GPP, mental stress, or physical pain.

To summarize, maximal strength is most important for the sprinter athletes. Those who are best at doing higher repetitions are best at longer distances. For one to excel in a certain distance, or sport, they will undoubtedly be gifted with one of three muscle types. The weightlifter or sprinter will have a higher degree of type IIB muscle fibers. On the other hand, soccer players, rugby players, and wrestlers, will have more type IIA muscle fibers. The type IIA fibers can be trained to perform, to some lesser extent, strength or endurance, depending on what is needed.

One last note, the sprinter must gain strength without adding mass. This means they must concentrate on maximal effort work. Resistance is determined by the amount of repetitions done in one set.

> For the most powerful athletes:
> Maximal effort—one repetition
> Submaximal effort—two or three repetitions
> Heavy resistance—four to seven repetitions
>
> For the endurance athletes:
> Moderate resistance—13 to 18 repetitions
> Light resistance—19 to 25 repetitions
> Very high resistance—over 25 repetitions
>
> These systems are according to Naglak (1979). More can be found in *Science of Sports Training*, Thomas Kurz (2001).

And lastly, know what event you are training for. Is it for 100 meters, or 42,195 meters, or a marathon? Although a 100-meter sprinter must possess some amount of speed endurance during the top speed maintenance phase, consider that the marathon runner might have to sprint to the finish line.

CHAPTER 16

SPECIAL WEIGHT TRAINING FOR LONG DISTANCE

Long distance meaning 20,000 meters or longer.

The long distance athlete must constantly increase their ability to perform work or exercises of low intensity for a very long duration, while exercising most of the muscles of the body, based on the level of their aerobic fitness. Years ago, Frank Shorter would better his times when he could perform more reps with 100-pound squats. The squat works most of the muscles of the body, so it is perfect for building general endurance. In order to increase endurance, one must work through fatigue. While this is something that commonly occurs while running, so does the deterioration of one's form. This can affect your time because of injuries. This is why special exercises must be included in your preparation for long distance running.

First, the ultra-distance runner must possess mostly type I fibers. The greatest long distance runners have about 70 percent type I fibers. Westside, for example, had a long distance female runner who had a max squat of 100 pounds, but could squat 65 pounds for 65 reps. It is very important for the long distance runner to increase their maximum strength, without the cost of a gain in bodyweight. Remember, any athlete's enemy is the force of gravity. Newton's Law of Gravity states that every object in the universe attracts every other object in the universe with a force proportional to the objects' masses and inversely proportional to the square of the distance between their centers, $F - (m_1 \times m_2)/d_2$. By becoming stronger and being able to display more muscle power, one can reduce ground contact time. This holds true not only for the sprinter, but the long distance runner as well. While building the major muscle groups for running, the lower leg muscles are often completely neglected. Of great importance is the development of the push-off force from the ankle joint. This requires strong calf muscles. This may be done in several ways such as standing and seated calf raises, for example. Seated with legs kept straight is best performed in a plyo-swing for explosive strength, with low reps. To increase strength endurance, the athlete must use very high reps, about 50 to 70 reps per set, performing a total of about 25 reps.

For strength endurance, start with either regular squats or box squats. Perform sets of 120 reps, for two to five sets, depending on the athlete's level of preparedness. A regular bar can be used for the front and back squats. Back squats are best, as they place emphasis on the hips and hamstrings. The quads are breaking muscles and the hamstrings are for pulling forward. Switch the type of bar used when squatting on a regular basis, for example a cambered bar or the safety squat bar, and, of course, the belt squat machine, which is great for back traction.

The Safety Squat Bar

A safety squat bar is excellent for walking long distances. Not only does this improve leg and core strength, but it also greatly taxes the lungs, by sitting on the upper back. Walking intervals may be up to one mile for high level endurance training. Most can cover 400 meters in roughly four minutes, using weights ranging from just the bar, 75 pounds, to 135 pounds or even 175 pounds. Try intervals of 400 to 800 meters to start with. One must keep track of the weight and how long it took to cover the distance. It is most important to continue using the same method of walking. It must be as energetic as possible. Use three different weights to improve upon. Start with the largest weight early in the week, and reduce the weight throughout the week. A second method is to complete two trips with heavy weight, then reduce the weight and push for a new time record. This is known as contrast training. It is common to throw to heavy shot puts, then a lighter one on the third throw. Using lighter weights, or even just the bar, try running, but use caution and only run on good level surfaces. Remember to try for a timed record with a set weight every two or three weeks. A second method to help reduce the deceleration portion of a race is to choose a time—five, 10, or 15 minutes—to start. Then, try to cover a longer distance in the same time frame the next time. If you make a longer distance in a set time period, you have become more powerful and should be ready to run faster times, provided your running form is mastered.

The Sled

Powerwalking with a weight sled of three different weights can be used following the same method as the safety squat bar work. For the weight sled, two methods are recommended. First, use long strides landing on the heels. Upon touching the surface, react with powerful pulling using the calves and hamstrings. The second method is slow motion running using the same mechanisms as running, touching the ball of the foot first. Note: this is powerwalking, where both feet are in contact with the track, or any other surface.

The Wheelbarrow Push or Pull

A strongman wheelbarrow is pushed or pulled for building strength speed endurance for exercises up to 800 meters. This not only builds all muscles that are required for running or sprinting, but also develops balance for any distances. Pulling it like a rickshaw will build the posterior chain very effectively. Again, use three different weights to break speed or distance records.

Why is this type of work important to the runner of all distances? The legs work like springs, the more force applied to the ground, the further they push the sprinter, or any runner, forward. Any one athlete is only so strong and only weighs so much, therefore they are limited to how much power or force they can produce while running. Here lies the reason to use resistance training. No one can lift a heavy weight slowly, they lift it as fast as possible. This causes the athlete to develop maximal force while exerting force. Remember the definition of work, $W=Fd$, and then define power, $P=W/T$. If any distance is defined as work, and it should be, then the most powerful athlete will cover that distance in a shorter time. This is basic physics. It is true that the average person applies 500 to 600 pounds of force when running. And the top sprinters sometimes apply more than 1,000 pounds per step. It is due to their strength to bodyweight ratio that makes it possible for them to apply such a great force. To this end, a major weapon at Westside is the belt squat machine.

THE BELT SQUAT MACHINE

This machine allows the athlete to stand, squat, walk, or run in place with resistance attached around the waist by the use of a belt. First, let's look at belt squatting. Use a box with a cushion on top that can range from parallel to several inches above parallel. The method: perform a very fast eccentric phase and bounce off of the cushion to stand in a very rhythmic manner. For maintaining top speed for strength endurance, perform one rep per second for as long as possible. The athlete must maintain this pace for at least one minute. Two minutes should be easy to maintain for most advanced runners. If one is able to maintain a pace and time suitable to the athlete, add a small amount of weight. If ten pounds is added for one minute, 600 pounds of additional work will be done in the same time frame. Additionally, simple math shows that in two minutes, 1,200 pounds of added work is done. This cannot be done with regular running. As one progresses to five- minute intervals, add five or ten more pounds. Most can start out with one 45-pound plate. For over speed eccentrics, replace the weight plates with rubber bands around the weight holders. The bands will force the athlete down much faster, causing an increase in KE stored in the lower limbs. This will produce a stronger stretch reflex and can make one able to run much faster or longer due to better locomotion.

Next, we look at running in the belt squat machine. Attach rubber bands around the weight holder. Do not use plates. These bands work much like the human body, they stretch and contract. One may run in place for a set time. Try to maintain a set pace for long distance runners. Fifteen to 30 minutes, or any amount of time desired, may be used. Even 60 minutes can be done by advanced runners of five, 10, and 20,000 meters. For the less advanced, use time intervals like two at seven and a half minutes for 5,000 meters, or two at 15 minutes for a 10,000 meter race. For a 20,000 meter race, use four 15-minute or two 30-minute intervals. Always wave the workout using a three-week wave. Then, start over with a small increase in resistance.

A second method to calculate work is to simply count the steps of the athlete at any time interval. This system builds not only strength endurance, but explosive power, for much shorter runs like 100, 200, even up to 800. This would require the athlete to go all out for two minutes, for a top 800-meter runner. Just running alone will cause a speed barrier to interfere with further progress, by consistently repeating the same work over time. After all, the athlete must incorporate special strength starting with the maximal effort method.

The Maximal Effort Method

The body will respond to the demands placed upon it. This method will make one the strongest possible, due to activating the most muscle units (MU), and with optimal discharge frequency. Next is the dynamic method.

The Dynamic Method

Here, one must move or lift a non-maximal load with the fastest speed possible. One should use 30 percent to 40 percent for explosive speed, and 75 percent to 85 percent for speed strength. And, finally, the repeated or repetition method.

The Repeated/Repetition Method

With the Repeated/Repetition Method one lifts a submaximal weight till failure, or near failure, in small special exercises.

The athlete needs to build explosive strength or power. Explosive strength is the ability to rapidly increase force. The steeper the increase of strength in time, the greater the explosive strength (Tidow, 1990).

The Use of Exercises

It has been proven that strength training has no adverse effects on coordination or technique. This leads to two different methods of exercise. General strength training will allow one to move on to directed and sport-specific exercises for developing all major muscle groups that surround all joints in a balanced way. General exercises will help prevent most injuries.

CHAPTER 17

THE SPEED BARRIER

Thomas Kurz talks a lot about the speed barrier. What is the speed barrier? It is when one cannot run any faster, at any distance. What causes this? The speed barrier occurs when the coach's plan is basically repeated over and over, doing the same exercises and the same volume and intensity, and most of all, excessive amounts of running. How do we fix this? There are many special methods to build strength in the running muscles. An example is walking in a belt squat for time intervals that stimulate the race time. The shorter the race, the heavier the resistance should be. If one runs 400 meters, they should work for one minute with resistance through which they can maintain a moderate pace. The exercise should not tax ones aerobic fitness, but rather build the running muscle groups. As the muscles grow stronger, it allows the body to become more explosive for jumping exercises. Exercises for the posterior chain, such as glute-ham raises, inverse leg curls, plyometric swing bounding, and reverse hypers, make it possible to produce greater force on each and every ground contact and the jumping will reduce ground contact time. Squats, deadlifts, and power cleans will build greater strength for running any distance, but their success lies in their development through employing small special exercises. What lifts the leg? The hamstrings and calves, along with the hip muscles lift the leg. This process of building these two prime muscle groups will prevent many injuries. You might run with rubber bands held by a trainer, or walk with heavy weight, or sprint with a sled. Also effective are high rep lifting on squats, pulls, or weight jumps with 30 percent of a one rep max.

The speed barrier is also the definition of the Law of Accommodation. Both of which simply state that if you repeat the same training over and over again, you will detrain, meaning progress will stop and you will begin to run slower. This happens in all aspects of training, not only in a special strength, but also reaction time and flexibility. It is suggested that one cut running down a considerable amount, sometimes up to 35 percent. Once you learn to run correctly, the only way to run faster or longer is to become stronger. It is known that a sprinter relies on muscular power rather than the amount of fitness they possess. When running a very long distance, even a marathon, often the top runner's legs will give out. Sometimes even they have to sprint to the finish line. One must use directed and general speed and strength work for a majority of their training. Then, and only then, can one begin to make progress again.

RESTORATION FOR SPRINTERS

It seems coaches have forgotten the value of rest and restoration methods. The author constantly sends sprinters out of Westside to college on a full-ride scholarship, just to watch as they slow down and then become injured. How? Too much running, incorrect weight training and little rest. More is not better without more rest as well. Bodybuilding is not made for running faster or jumping higher. If a good coach has a great program, they should do it along with the team. But, it is not always a good program, rather a program of unspecific work that leads to no progress and injuries that the athlete is somehow held accountable for. I do not believe these bad coaches will be offended by this because I am sure they do not read any books at all, but rather follow the poor training advice of their predecessors.

It is easy to over train the lower body during running and hurdling. This is often due to the balance between the anterior quadriceps femurs and the posterior hamstring groups. At Westside, a female lifter and sprinter, Laura Dodd, had a quad to hamstring ratio of 40 percent quad, 60 percent hamstring. To my knowledge, this is the highest ratio of its kind ever recorded. It is more commonly the exact opposite. Westside does not experience hamstring injuries. Why does it happen after leaving Westside and entering track practice? The coach, more often than not, uses the front squat as a major training aid for running. This is another major mistake. Why? When the quads become stronger, they contract harder, keeping the hamstrings from being able to relax, which then causes many injuries.

Other reasons can be a low base strength due to the wrong exercises mentioned above, low physical preparedness, and a poor diet. We suggest 200 ankle weight leg curls per day for a low intensity conditioning of the hamstrings. It is most important for the coach to choose the right workload for each and every one on the track, as well as the correct special exercises. If one is overly fatigued, use longer rest intervals and change the group of special exercises being used currently with other special exercises that work the same muscle groups in a slightly different way in order to avoid accommodation.

Never train with a serious injury. This can lead to more serious injuries or even end a promising career. Because the hamstrings are most important, much attention must be paid to them. The coach should include all types of leg curls, standing, laying, glute-hams, inverse leg curls, ankle weight leg curls, and reverse hypers. These can be done during in season or after squatting or pulling exercises. We prefer to warm up with box jumps. The hamstrings can be made stronger by electro stimulation. Use caution on the type of contractions set forth on the device, they can be very strong. Other restoration methods may be sauna, ice bath, massage, and, of course, retaining adequate fluids. When pain occurs in the foot, calf, or Achilles tendon, active release therapy, also known as ART, should be introduced at least once per week. If pain from too much work arises, reduce training loads.

Use the three-week pendulum wave for all training, including sprinting and running of any distance, not just for weight training. Increase the work over the three weeks. Then, drop the amount, in terms of mileage, to just slightly above the previous week one and start the wave over according to the level of preparedness of the individual athlete.

Nutrition is a vital part of training as well. It must contain vitamins, minerals, and protein. Also explore pharmacological preparations. For strong muscle contractions needed for the 60, 100, 200, and 400 meter runners, pay close attention to the level of creatine phosphate reserved in the muscles.

Of course, the feet are very important for running. Proper shoes must be worn while training. Running in sand, exercising barefoot in grass, foot massages, and electro stimulation can be used throughout the year. Overtraining can be detected by a decrease in work capacity and technical breakdown in running or jumping form. These are just a few things a coach must consider.

If a young boy or girl wants to become a top sprinter, he or she must start as early as eight to 11 years of age. A large amount of base work should begin at 12- to 14-years-old. Remember, a pyramid is only as tall as its base allows it to be. At 15 or 16 years of age, one must start specialization, meaning choosing the events you will compete in. Do not compete in an event just to fill a void on the team. This will highly interfere with the next step, which is deep specialization. Deep specialization begins at 17 to 20 years of age. These guidelines were set forth by age, maturity, and motor skill development. Don't be discouraged by your progress, as at times progress can be faster or slower for different periods. Of course, there must be good coaching at the top level, but it is also important in the beginning as to ensure the correct direction in which the child is progressing. Are they gaining strength and technique as well as building a continuously larger work capacity? The child must not only be taught what to do, but also why it is taught. After all, they may become coaches one day as well.

Always track progress, not only on the track, but also in the weight room, while jumping, and so forth. Also, note what types of restoration works best for the specific athlete. If the weight periodization laid out in the book is closely followed correctly, men and women will be able to train without overtraining. It is based on their own strength potential, as well as their jumping ability.

REACTIVE METHODS PLUS CONTRAST METHODS

Reactive methods must be made available to the athlete to develop power and explosive strength by specific demands on the central nervous system. Plyometrics are commonly used for explosive power development. But, there are many other reactive methods to use as well. These methods are referred to as contrast methods.

Y. Verkhoshansky and A. Bondarchuk suggest combinations of large weights first, then smaller weights after to cause a contrast method. A weight of at least 90 percent for a few repetitions, then small weights, around 30 percent of one rep max for repetitions until the movement speed is slowed. This causes an adaptive reaction to the body over time. Three sets of large weights—at least 90 percent of one rep max—and two sets of small weights, around 30 percent, for eight to10 repetitions, accentuating explosive power. One should never sit when training. Rather, do exercises for flexibility, or even include a short jog. The purpose of such contrast methods are to increase general jumping ability.

At eight- to 11-years-old, general exercise and games GPP should be implemented as well as a weight sled with light weights for short 60 to 800 meter walks. Kneeling jumps, at age eight, are introduced for strength, power, and coordination. Up to 40 jumps, two times per week, are recommended. Use gym mats while doing jumps off of the knees. The author has always sought the advice of sports scientists in their respective fields and József Drabik, PhD, is no exception. He calls for jumping ropes, short jogging, bounding around a track, walking lunges, riding bikes, sitting down and standing up without using your hands, pushups beginning with half pushups, throwing balls, catching balls, and moving on the hitting of a slow pitch and then increasing the speed of the pitch, shooting a basketball or kicking a soccer ball as well. There is much to learn from Drabik's book, *Children and Sports Training*.

SPECIAL STRENGTH DEVELOPMENT

After learning proper strength technique, you must learn what muscles are responsible for increasing speed. One must consider the shin muscles and how they are developed. It is generally known that different jumps, hops, and calf raises can aid in their speed strength preparation, increasing stride frequency through multi jumps. Reverse calf raises, in which you raise onto the balls of your feet, will aid as well. This separates the top sprinter from low level sprinters, and comes from great strength and coordination from the hip muscles. It will occur when more special strength work for the sprinting muscles are provided for the athlete, which will require coaches to implement less running, while adding special exercises for the glutes, hamstrings, calves, and thighs. It does no good to be strong in the wrong muscles. However, this does not mean to do bodybuilding exercises, but rather special strength exercises many times on different special devices.

Before selecting the special exercises, one must look at the development between corresponding muscle groups for sprinters. Here is a short list:

Leg Curl	Standing Leg Curl
Calf-Glute-Ham	Reverse Hyper
Inverse Leg Curl	Back Raise
Goodmorning	Leg Extension
Leg Raise	Weight on Swing Leg
Box Squat	Belt Squat
Standing Calf Raise	Seated Calf Raise

The great V. Borozov, when asked what he needed in training, would reply "Make it harder." By this he means adding special jumps and weight exercises, such as the calf-glute-ham raises. When sprinting with light weight on a sled, a powerful extension of the legs must be realized by the activation of the glute muscles. This can be done with very heavy isolated reverse hypers on a step machine. While doing so, keep the feet, heels, and toes held tightly together with a foam roller of about five-inch circumference held inside the thighs. This aids greatly in adding muscle tension in the glutes and hamstrings, as well as the adductors. Add to this knee extensions.

Being stronger will not only aid in being more powerful in the start and acceleration phases, but also in all phases of sprinting: the start, the acceleration, and the maintenance of top speed. Perfect technique must be explained and practiced by the coach to the sprinter. But, many times a lack of strength in just one muscle group may distract one's technique. Remember, for a sprinter, it is necessary to show maximum strength in the shortest possible time. A muscle group that is often neglected is the lower leg muscles including the soles, the skin muscles, and the gastrocnemius, which is the chief muscle of the calf of the leg that flexes the knee and foot. It runs to the Achilles tendon from two heads attached to the femur. These muscles stretch and take up energy that can contribute to the takeoff phase.

This brings us to the conclusion that the coach must prescribe specific resistance training for the precise running muscles. For sprinting, one must build maximum muscle strength by the ME method. Raising maximum muscle strength will bring forth the highest degree of speed and explosive strength qualities in the sprinter as well as longer distance runners.

While training for speed strength and explosive strength at 75 to 85 percent for speed strength and roughly 30 percent for explosive strength, the stronger the athlete, the larger the weights needed to develop speed and explosive strength. For example, a 300-pound squatter would train for explosive strength at 30 percent, which would represent 90 pounds for jumping squats. The bar speed would be at least $1\text{-}1.3^{m}/_{s}$. A 500-pound squatter would train for explosive strength at 30 percent, which equates to 150 pounds. The bar speed would be the same for the model athlete, $1\text{-}1.3^{m}/_{s}$. This is made possible by the periodization that Westside presents in the periodization section beginning on Page 10.

We have talked about the impact on the shins and calf muscles. Focusing on the calf muscles allowed a Big Ten 60-meter champion's 100 meter time to move from 10.47 to 10.17, in just nine weeks, after the top sprint coach said he could not run any faster. He came to me and I started having him do specialized strength training for the sprinting muscles, starting with the lower legs and lots of seated calf raises. Seated calf work was done primarily due to the fact that most of the calf work is done while running. But, you must train the entire calf, including the front of the shins. Very fast reps were done. Basically, by flexing concentrically, and dropping eccentrically, setting a stretch reflex action. Explosive and strength endurance was developed with not only the fast repetitions, but also the high number of repetitions performed. Ten reps with 50 pounds, then a fast load to 75 pounds, 100 pounds, 125 pounds, then deload to 100 pounds, 75 pounds., and back to 50 pounds as fast as possible. Three workouts per week for explosive calves, plus tibia raises were also used to combat shin splints. Do not neglect the calves. Thighs were trained with thigh extensions with isometric holds for approximately 15 seconds at completion. This is done because when landing on depth jumps or while landing on the track, thigh muscles contract isometrically for a brief moment between the eccentric and concentric phases. **Without a plan, you plan to fail**.

The coach must take preventative measures to prevent injuries that could keep the athlete off the track. Possibly forever.

BAD EXAMPLES

Westside prepared two top female prospects for two major colleges. One with a 7.20 60-meter and a 23.85 200-meter, only to slow down until sidelined by major chronic shin and hamstring injuries. This was due to severe overtraining by a bad coach who obviously never read a book by top track coaches.

The second female sprinter, with almost equal times, became slower and slower after going to college, somewhat due to gaining too much weight. This was unexpected, to say the least. This sprinter had a 50½-inch box jump at 17-years-old, while training at Westside. One explanation the coach had was that she lacked elastic energy while running. But, the coach had zero jumping employed into her training program. This is a bad coach that has read just enough to get into trouble. All coaches should know that minimal ground contact, or increasing elastic energy, comes from jumping, bounding, and depth jumps from the appropriate heights for the level of preparedness of the athlete.

The two female sprinters were trained at Westside Barbell and made their fastest running times while training at Westside, where they were taught the value of special strengths and the velocity at which they are trained. Please, coach, read the work of top coaches and use the right equipment. Don't rely on top recruiting alone. To develop better athletes, you must become a better coach.

Let's get back to the nine-week training that reduced the Big Ten, 60-meter sprint champ's time from 10.47 to 10.17. Next, the hamstrings were trained with glute-ham raises. First, he did 12 to 15 reps with weight to condition the entire hamstring. Then, lower reps were performed for maximum strength. The reps were six to eight, keeping tension on the hamstrings for longer than 10 seconds, or the time in which he covered the 100 meter. This athlete had a 450-pound box squat for a one rep max. He used a three-week pendulum wave with 50 to 60 percent, for five sets of five reps, with 25 percent band tension at lockout.

Next up, reverse hypers. His squat volume for speed strength was 5,400 pounds. It made his reverse hyper volume, with 50 percent of his top box squat, roughly 20,000 pounds. This work is completely directed for the hamstrings, glutes, hips, and low back. A strong low back will prevent hamstring pulls. The reverse hypers work as not only a range of motion machine, but also a strength builder, and finally, a traction device for the spine and connective tissues.

Next on the list were belt squats. In this manner, the belt squats were done for sets. The sprinter could do 12 reps in 12 seconds with a single 45-pound plate. During the nine weeks, he increased his strength and power to the point of doing 12 reps in 12 seconds with 135 pounds. This carried over to the track.

We simply increased the amount of work able to be done in the same set time period. This is simple. Work is defined as the product of net force and the displacement through which that force is exerted, or, $W=Fd$. Power is defined as work done divided by the time used to do the work, or $P=W/T$. What does this mean to your athlete? It means that the most powerful one can run the same distance in a faster time.

This left power sled walking and acceleration work with the sled. On Mondays, he would pull a very heavy sled, with weights ranging from 225 pounds in the beginning, to 315 pounds after nine weeks. The distance was 60 meters, as powerful as possible, while over striding and touching the heel first. This builds strength in the entire posterior chain, also including the feet. On Wednesdays, the weight was reduced to 180 pounds, or close to bodyweight. This was also done for 60 meters. The bodyweight sled work is meant to aid in maintaining top speed endurance. One must never be lazy when powerwalking, rather create as much force as possible with each step. On Fridays, the sled work was done for acceleration. He used 45 pounds and used his sprinting technique. After a warm up, six to eight sprints were done.

This leaves box jumps. No depth jumps were performed. We did only kneeling jumps and jumps up onto boxes. As his jump height increased, his sprint time went down. Sixty jumps were done three times per week. On the third week, he did jumping with only bodyweight. This is wave periodization for jumping. Most jumps, however, were done with Kettlebells, a weight vest, and ankle weights.

This is a simple program that, with short rest intervals, takes no longer than 45 to 60 minutes, even for the strongest sprinters. A coach must realize that weight training is much more than bars and plates, but rather physics, biomechanics, and mathematics. There is much to learn and read from experts that combined both, such as Verkhoshansky and Bondarchuk, just to name a few.

Westside has produced not only the strongest, but some of the fastest and most explosive, athletes on earth. As your athletes become stronger, they will, of course, change to some extent. First, exercises for the improvement of flexibility and mobility of the soft tissue and muscles and joints must be included in the weekly plan. All sports require these three components. It allows for full range of motion movements. To be strong one must be flexible, and to be flexible one must be strong. Look at your event, and your training should be aimed at specialization. Almost all weight exercises can help increase mobility in the joints, like a lower and lower box squat as well as going wider and wider, using a cambered bench bar, or just benching with a much wider grip. Using one dumbbell at a time can increase range of motion. The coach and athlete must pay attention to the Law of Accentuation. This means to work the range of motion of the main sport movement, where the demand for high force production is maximal. Maximal muscle contractions happen at the extreme points of angular motion. More on this can be found in *Science and Practice of Sports Training* by V. Zatsiorsky.

Westside uses a delayed transformation system to increase sports performance. While this system was designed to stop doing a lift or an event completely and replace it with special exercises, small and large, or special drills instead of the events of long jump, or shot put. But, this can lead to being much more proficient in the drills or special exercises with no improvement in the lift or event. Westside prescribes to rotate more special exercises or drills that are close to the competitive lift or event. For example, doing a box or rack deadlift, or sometimes using bands for accommodation, but never doing the actual deadlift. Or, use 10 and 20 meter starts, or flying starts from 40 to 60 meters to the completion of your sprint. What is described above is for a large base to train from. Remember, the larger the base, the higher the pyramid. This reduces the chance of injuries and adds to the chance that you will better your sport's results.

The coach must be willing to reduce running by roughly 25 percent and allow the athlete to use the Conjugate Westside System. Inverse curls can be done for two to six reps for maximal strength or 200 reps in the ankle weights. Leg curls can be done as rehab by not only building strong muscles, but also building durable and elastic ligaments, which prevents injuries. One must use many exercises that are done in a somewhat different angle. Weights are best in most cases, as a machine will build strength, but not motion. Many athletes have poor posture due to a weak torso, meaning the front and side abs, as well as the entire back. If the athlete has an unequal balance this may cause injuries or hinder performance at the very least. A person can move in almost every direction, so you must exercise in almost every direction. The coach must learn the proper form of all weighted exercises. (Caution: do not body build, rather, as the author related to running fast, build the muscles that run.) Use low reps with a barbell and very high reps with small weights or special machines. If your athlete is underweight, use a barbell for five to six reps at 70 percent. This percentage should be able to be moved rather fast in most barbell exercises. Use the volume that is recommended in the periodization section. If your athlete is somewhat overweight, replace a portion of the weight training with more jumping.

While talking at a seminar in Las Vegas around 1998, Dr. Mel Siff said to our guests, "One should never train minimally, nor should one train maximally, but rather optimally." Mel and the author have spent countless hours discussing all types of training, but that statement has had the most profound effect on the Westside system. The author had read many charts that had a maximal, minimal, and optimal amounts of sets, reps, and number of different lifts that should be performed at a certain percentage, or how often to do large, medium, or small workouts. But, in Las Vegas in 1998, Mel got it in my mind. There are many things that should stay in Vegas, but optimal training is not one of them. This coach means not to run your athletes into the ground, but have them train optimally according to their level of preparedness. If your program is that good, you and your assistant coaches should train along with the athletes and test its merits for yourself. Remember, you can cut a chicken's head off and it can still run. So, only running is not the answer. The answer is a complete collection of training with special exercises to develop special track skills.

CHAPTER 18

Jamaican Secrets or System?

The last decade has seen the Jamaicans dominate the world of sprinting. How? Do they have secrets about sprinting that the others don't know? This could be true, but only because they understand the sprinter like no one else.

What are the facts?

First, it is selection. For such a small island to possess such a great sprinting talent, it is, of course, genetics. To be the very best at sprinting, one must be dominant with type IIB fibers or fast twitch fibers. This is, of course, fast motor units as they provide maximal force. Also, they have maximal speed of contraction causing great strength. To make them gain greater force, Maximal Effort weight training must be incorporated. This process is referred to as myofibrillar hypertrophy. Maximal Effort method means one rep max.

Doing two or three reps at weights, about 90 percent of a one rep max, builds strength endurance. Remember, to define a sprint is to run as fast as possible for a short distance. Their coaches realize a sprinter must be strong and powerful, but relaxed. It is easy to see the typical Jamaican is at ease while competing at the highest level. Their top sprinters are very extraverted. The sports observer sees this in all sports. The most outgoing are always the most explosive. It is, for a large part, a poor country and one way to gain wealth and fame is to run. To this point, it is clear the selection is very important for success. You will never see a jackass win a horse race.

Coaching is a major factor in their world dominance. Their coaches understand it does no good to be strong in the wrong drill or weight training. First, they work to perfect correct form while sprinting. It is taught by Coach Glen Mills who was greatly influenced by the renowned Bub Winters' programming. Everyone has potential, but only a great coach can get it out of a great sprinter.

Their coaches are the boss, but at the same time, must adapt to the sprinters emotional status. Never let the sprinter lose direction of their short and long term goals. The coach knows how to address technical problems—to address mechanical short comings. These problems can lead to career ending injuries. They understand the importance of a strong torso to allow proper lean for optimal sprinting. This can greatly reduce stress on the posterior chain including the lower back that can lead to hamstring injuries.

Their coaches must understand when to push and when to ease up when the sprinters are not themselves. A good coach must look at a long-term plan and not for just the next race. Their coaches know how to train for a certain distance—and the importance of recovery. And above all, to keep on a pace to succeed ... meaning not to fall behind or get too far ahead in training.

There must be a solid base of training to rely on. Going too fast without a large base can cause failure. Remember, the coaches say it is not all physical, but also mental. The sprinter must have rivalry, even if it is his or her own times. Top sprinters have acceleration up to 65 meters or 65 percent of 100 meters. They can maintain top speed for 18 meters and then decelerate for the final 12 meters. Remember, the winner does not go faster at the finish line, but rather the losers slow down more than the winner. They run 300 meters to build speed endurance as well as train to accelerate for a longer period of time. If one looks at Charlie Francis's method, he felt one must build pure speed. When one looks at Ben Johnson's training, he constantly was able to accelerate for a longer time up to 70 meters —and his best.

As this longer acceleration phase was built, he became more dominant. One drill for the Jamaicans is to run 60 meters and walk for 45 meters and repeat in an interval method. This can be found in the book *Bolt Supremacy* by Richard Moore. Like Westside, weight sled for the purpose of acceleration is done 20 percent of body weight mostly on grass. By many tests at Westside, weight sleds with body weight will maintain top speed endurance. By adding up the two types of weight sleds work, it covers 83 percent of a sprint. This is a plan and that is what the Jamaicans have ... a plan, great selection due to the body type and muscle fiber, plus an emotional, fun-loving, no pressure group of athletes that love their tiny country.

It's not secret drugs or super advanced training laid out by great coaches like Glen Mills. It takes work and pride to be a champ. It is no secret that the Jamaicans rule the world of sprinting ... it's just a system.

What is, and How to Use, Accommodation Resistance

The idea of Accommodation Resistance is to provide maximal tension throughout the entire range of motion. Everyone recalls the Nautilus of the 1970s, with its special cam design. Long before Arthur Jones' innovation, Gustaf Zander introduced the very same concept in 1879 to maximize accommodation.

One method to do this was an isokinetic rack, where the speed of movement concentrically was constant. This is referred to as mechanical feedback. This resistance is at a constant speed and is equal to the muscular force the athlete applies to the device. It makes it possible to attain high velocity, while producing small force. [See Hill equation of muscle contraction (*Super Training*, P. 145). Also, see the force-velocity relation curve in *Science and Practice of Strength Training*, P. 29-33.]

There is a much better way based on elasticity of rubber bands and its range of displacement. As one applies force to the bands, it stretches due to the force applied to it. The author is credited with the invention of the concept of Combinations of Resistance methods (*Super Training*, P. 409). In this method, chains and/or elastic bands are attached to the barbell to accommodate resistance. There is a formula for this: F=KD, where F is force, and k is a coefficient (stiffness), and D is deformation. The key word here is deformation. The greater the range of stretch on the band, the greater the muscle force is needed. By adding bands to the barbell, it will accommodate the strength curve.

Another method is the Peak Contraction Principle, where the main effort is to apply force to the weakest points of the human strength curve. The third method is Accentuation. This method's main objective is to train strength only in the range of the main sport movement where high force production is maximal. Rubber bands combined with a barbell of different percentages also produce a faster eccentric phase that contributes to reversible muscular action known as the stretch shortening cycle. That makes it possible for a faster concentric phase.

The stretch shortening cycle can be explained by dropping a rubber ball to the ground and watching how high it bounces back upward. Next, throw the same ball down by force and watch how much higher it bounces upward than the ball that was dropped at 9.8 meters per second —which is the speed of acceleration of gravity on earth. The ball does not have a central nervous system, but it bounces upward faster as the eccentric phase is faster. This is also the case of using rubber bands over the barbell, forcing the athlete to increase their eccentric phase that in turn increases the concentric phase.

Why do rubber bands work so well for building special strength, meaning explosive speed and strength speed? It is because they work like the muscles and tendons. They stretch and contract, plus the elastic energy is proportional to the applied force that causes deformation.

When running at higher and higher speeds, you have a greater deformation that causes greater power output. This is because of an increase in Kinetic Energy (KE = ½mv²).

To increase Kinetic Energy, it is better to have higher velocity than mass. This also can be looked at as Newton's Second Law. And speaking of physics, playing a great role is running. We must look at Newton's Third Law, when object X exerts a force on object Y, then object Y exerts an equal and opposite force on X. This is what happens during the stretch-shortening cycle during the support period in running.

Does Accommodation Resistance work? In an experiment on barbell weight versus combinations of resistance methods, the author, along with the assistance of calculus professor Dr. Akita, used Matt Smith as a subject to do three singles with 550 pounds on a parallel box. The eccentric and concentric phase was timed at a ninth of a second.

Bar weight was removed and rubber bands were added, making the top value 750 pounds. While sitting on the box with zero velocity it was 550 pounds, same as with just the barbell weight. But this time, the subject was timed at 5.4 and 5.7 seconds on the eccentric and concentric phase.

How did he move 200 pounds more through the same range of motion in over three-tenths of a second faster? The answer is over speed eccentrics. It is much like a world class sprinter whose body weight is normally 220 pounds, but produces 1,000 pounds of force on each step by striking the ground as fast as possible. And what happens when this happens? You have deformation equal to the force applied, and consequently, an opposite force concentrically occurs causing very minimal ground contact. While chains on the barbell will cause accommodation resistance on the concentric phase, the rubber bands provide the over speed eccentric phase that provided added speed on the concentric phase.

What is a virtual force? Virtual force is a force that is present, but not recognized. One can walk on thin ice but not jump on thin ice without going through. This is an example of a virtual force. Why can a fat runner run a long distance with little muscle mass? Because the elastic energy is stored in the tendons and is recycled from human locomotion.

These tendons work much like springs that can store and recoil a large amount of mechanical energy as each set is delivered. We know that the stretch reflex is very important when a muscle is stretched. It is activated to combat the deformation force. The Golgi tendon organ's reflex is a safeguard to prevent high force that can cause injury to the muscle and tendons. But remember, when you drop a rubber ball, it bounces back upward due to the opposite force it achieved from falling at 9.8 meters per second.

And when one throws the rubber ball downward at a fast rate of speed, it bounces back much higher, also due to its opposite and equal effect. In both instances, the ball has no brain or central nervous system. Its cause and effect is due to the person's effort to drop or throw the rubber ball downward.

The same is true when using rubber bands attached to the barbell. The bands force the barbell eccentric phase at a faster rate of speed that, in turn, is recognized in the muscles and tendons. Why can depth jumps be dangerous? Because if one free falls from a high position, motion velocity is added to the body causing a greater impact force as the fall becomes higher and higher due to the kinetic energy on impact. The fall through space dictates the force upon impact. This is just one reason to add accommodated resistance in the form of rubber bands.

When jumping, sprinting, or lifting a weight through a set distance, it is a form of work. In physics, work is defined as the product of the net force and the displacement through which that force is exerted, or $W = FD$. Now, let's look at power. Power is defined as work done, divided by the time used to do the work, or $P = WT$. The end result is that the more powerful he or she becomes, the more work the athlete can do in less time … and that means winning.

If you remember the experiment by the author and Dr. Akita, it should make sense to use over speed eccentric training. It has also been said that muscles grow stronger at a faster rate than tendons and ligaments. This is true when using weights only and by using rubber bands at a fast rate of speed. During the reversible phase, the shock absorption phase is created in the soft tissue. This is all about creating a pre-stretch in the muscles and tendons. This brings us back to how basic physics is involved in the task of sports excellence.

First, look at collisions. We are talking about when the runner's foot comes in contact with the track. When one foot comes in contact, its force —whatever it is — will be equal to the take-off phase until physical fatigue overcomes the runner. Remember, the amount of stored energy is proportional to the applied force that caused deformation. Now let's compare this to Hooke's Law of Elasticity. Hooke's Law states that the amount of deformation produced by a force is proportional to the amount of force. The human does not obey Hooke's Law completely, again due to losing muscular force due to some degree of fatigue. So, why does accommodation resistance with rubber bands work so well? It works because the rubber bands pre-load the muscle and tendons by supplying over speed eccentrics. This causes a much greater stretch reflex. Other band exercises, like band leg curls while sitting or standing do the same. The method is to let the band powerfully extend the hamstrings, then reverse the action as fast as possible to activate the tendons —much like the support phase in running. All types of hamstring exercises must be rotated often to avoid accommodation.

What is the best hamstring exercises and why? The inverse curl is very effective due to its design that allows an eccentric phase first to maximize the pre-loading of the hamstrings. I hope the reader can see the relationship between accommodation resistance and physics. The term "Exercise Science" is just that, a term used at a university for a degree that one earns, having taken classes and passed with the grade received. But in reality, there is seldom any relationship between the two—exercise and applying science of some type. This is a mistake. Don't let this happen to you.

CHAPTER 19

WEIGHT PROGRAMS

One should train only one single strength in one workout. This refers to explosive strength, which is trained at a high velocity. Explosive strength training calls for weights ranging from 30 percent to 40 percent. The reps must stop when velocity slows. The steeper the increase of strength in time, the greater the explosive strength. The force-velocity relationship states that when maximum velocity is reached, the load will be small, meaning between 30 to 40 percent. The workout is always done within a three-week pendulum wave using 30 percent for week one, 35 percent for week two, and 40 percent for week three. This small increase in weight will eliminate accommodation. The rest interval between sets should allow for recovery. Accommodate a rest time of 90 seconds between the six to 10 sets of six reps. The amount of sets used is dependent on the individual athlete's sports preparedness.

Example:

Three Week Pendulum Waves

400-Pound Squat				
Week	Percentage	Weight	Sets	Reps
Week One	30%	120 lb.	6-10	6-10
Week Two	35%	140 lb.	6-10	6-10
Week Three	40%	160 lb.	6-10	6-10

500-Pound Squat				
Week	Percentage	Weight	Sets	Reps
Week One	30%	150 lb.	6-10	6-10
Week Two	35%	175 lb.	6-10	6-10
Week Three	40%	200 lb.	6-10	6-10

600-Pound Squat				
Week	**Percentage**	**Weight**	**Sets**	**Reps**
Week One	30%	180 lb.	6-10	6-10
Week Two	35%	210 lb.	6-10	6-10
Week Three	40%	240 lb.	6-10	6-10

This program is designed to increase the rate of force development, which is a must for high level performance in sports.

When choosing a sport for yourself or recruiting an athlete, you must have the correct muscle fiber to excel at sprinting or longer distance running. Type I muscle fibers, which are slow twitch or slow oxidation fibers, are resistant to fatigue. These fibers accommodate for long distance cycling, swimming, and running. A person with such muscle fibers will find it difficult to gain large amounts of muscle mass. The Type I fiber is good at doing very little making them suited for endurance training. For example, Westside trained a female long distance runner whose maximum squat was 100 pounds, yet she could do 100 reps with 65 pounds. She would never excel at sprinting or jumping. The explosive athlete must possess type IIB muscle fibers—fast twitch glycolytic muscle fibers. Type IIB muscle fibers are for maximal force production for sprinting or weightlifting, for example. These fibers can and will produce and increase in size and strength. The training must be of high intensities for best results, including box and vertical jumping. They are anaerobic. The intensities are high, above 75 percent to 100 percent plus. However, they should be done in low reps and high sets, as we are not building larger muscles, but rather stronger muscles. Westside says "Big ain't strong. Strong is strong." When trying to achieve faster leg and arm speed, greater results are made by lifting heavy weights, not light weights. The deadlift was shown to be the most effective lift for improving running speed. Westside uses the Sumo Style to deadlift, meaning hands inside the legs, for greater use of lower body strength, but also to safely build all the muscles above the waist.

After each three-week wave, go back to week one and use 30 percent. Also, it is advisable to rotate a different bar each wave. Example: front squat, back squat, Safety Squat Bar, 14-inch Cambered Bar, Bow Bar, etc. By rotating bars, the body is forced to adjust slightly due to the specific dynamics of the special bars. Belt squatting may also be introduced into the rotation and, by using a variety of box heights, will stimulate different muscle groups at different times during the lift. Always add two to four small special exercises for the running muscle groups. This is known as the Dynamic Method, which is used for the improvement of the rate of force development and explosive strength.

Speed Strength

The Dynamic Method is also used for speed strength. The weights are still submaximal at 75 percent, 80 percent, and 85 percent, in a three-week wave. The bar speed will be slower, about $.8-.9^{m}/_{s}$, compared to the speed of explosive strength which is $1^{m}/_{s}$ and up to $2.2^{m}/_{s}$. The sets are five to 12. The reps are three to six at 70 percent weights, and two to four at 80 percent weights. More reps at these percentages and the barbell will decelerate, losing force. These percentages build acceleration through Compensatory Acceleration Training, or CAT. A far superior method to eliminate bar deceleration was developed by the author and is known as Combinations of Resistance Methods. This consists of adding rubber bands, chains, or both to the barbell in order to accommodate resistance. Bands also add eccentric bar speed to contribute to the stretch reflex. It is recommended to use Accommodation Resistance (AC) on both explosive and speed strength. The number of reps at 70 percent is 12 minimum, 15 optimal, and around 20 maximum. For the five classical lifts—squat, bench, deadlift, clean, and snatch—the number of lifts must be used. Only 20 percent of the weight training is done with a barbell while 80 percent consists of small special exercises for both the upper and lower body. While explosive strength is trained at high velocity, speed strength is trained at intermediate velocity. This is due to the fact that as loads grow, velocity slows. Coaches have their ideas on how to run faster, but it comes down to greater ground force. This is physics. By constantly using the pendulum wave system you are strong and powerful all year long. Once you learn how to train correctly, you must become more powerful in order to run any distance faster. The waves should be rotated from explosive strength for three weeks.

All the training will be starting strength and accelerating strength. Do not use western periodization as it is a Dynamic Effort (DE) training system. After a phase of muscle building, then moving into a power development phase for a four- to six-week phase, you begin to lose the muscle mass you previously built. After moving to the strength phase for several weeks, you start to lose your power and muscle mass. Now you don't have a base of power or muscle to sustain the high volume high intensity training of both the weight room and the track. And, injuries happen. Is there a way to avoid this? You should use the Westside Conjugate System. It trains speed or explosive strength on one day, and top strength 72 hours later. For the upper and lower body, you have two dynamic workouts per week and two max effort workouts, twice per week, while doing small special exercises on all four workouts to build muscle mass, where and only where, it is needed. Plus, you have two extra workouts per week during the afternoon, or the next day. Extreme workouts, meaning high volume or high intensity, can be performed every 72 hours for the lower or upper body. Small workouts can be done every 12 or 24 hours, for a certain muscle restoration, or even flexibility or mobility. The weight workouts for most running athletes can be completed in 45 minutes or less. This can include jumping as well.

So far we have discussed how to be as explosive as possible through high velocity training with light weights and jumping, bounding, and depth jumps. Also, we have covered how to develop speed strength and acceleration abilities, using weights ranging from 75 percent to 85 percent, with the barbell or by using combinations of resistance methods, using chains and rubber bands to AC as well as providing over speed eccentrics. But, to increase the two above methods, there must be a third method.

Maximal Method

This method is done on max effort day for a one rep max where hopefully, an all-time record is obtained by a small margin. This method is sometimes called the Weight Lifting Method. The strength that is developed here is slow strength. It refers to the fact that velocity is slow to almost isometric where maximum strength is greatest. When velocity is small, force is great. To build strength speed, use a combination of bands and barbell weight with the band tension larger at the lockout than the amount on the barbell. Example: A 600-pound squat max could use 375 pounds of band tension and try to work up as high as possible with the barbell. With more band tension than barbell weight, the bands cause the bar to move slowly throughout the entire range of motion.

How accurate is this? Let's look at AJ Roberts' training cycle. During a strength speed cycle, AJ made 700 pounds of bands with 510 pounds of weight, equaling 1,210 pounds 21 days out from a meet, during circa-max training, AJ made 440 pounds of band tension with 740 pounds of barbell weight, equaling 1,180 pounds. At the contest, AJ made a 1,205-pound squat.

An individual only has one limit strength, but Westside has ways with the classical lifts to change the force-velocity curve, while maxing out with many combinations of resistance. The stronger one is, the faster one should be. This is why men out-run and out-jump women. This is a fact because men possess about 25 percent more muscle mass than women, therefore they can produce more force during ground contact. Heavy weight makes the limbs move faster, not light weight. For an example, have an athlete who can squat 600 pounds at a bodyweight of 200 pounds jump as high as possible. Now, have your athlete who can squat 200 pounds at a bodyweight of 200 pounds do the same, and see which athlete can jump the highest. I hope this makes sense to the coach. As one becomes stronger, you should not become slower if you combine the Dynamic Efforts Method along with the Max Effort Method during a weekly plan. No one can lift a heavy weight slow, you must apply maximum force throughout the entire range of motion. But anyone can lift a light weight slow, resulting from a small amount of force being applied to the barbell. All percentages of a one rep max must be lifted as fast as possible. Always remember, $F=MA$. This leads us to look at the differentiation of work. In physics, work is defined as the net force and the displacement through which that force is exerted, or, $W=Fd$. And that is true rather work is 60 meters or 200 meters.

Let's look at the definition of power as related to the athlete. Power is defined as work done divided by the time used to do the work, or $P=W/T$. Therefore, if two athletes run the same race, the more powerful one can do the work in less time. This is basic physics. Coaches, if you want to decrease your athletes' times in a race or increase the height or length of their jumps, you must first teach the skill, then make the athlete more powerful. We have already discussed more ME methods including forced repetitions or ballistics, where one lowers a weight as fast as possible onto the platform and bounces it back up sometimes onto foam blocks or rubber pads. Also, the Hoffman Method, where one pushes or pulls a bar from one position up to a second pin setting and exerting isometrics for one to six seconds. Remember, ME training is working up to a one rep max for that day, hopefully setting a new record by a small amount. Circa-max training calls for using weight in the 90 percent to 97 percent range for four to 10 lifts. Here, Westside uses seven lifts which are optimal at 90 percent plus, while working up to two sets of two reps, then three singles reaching a new record on the third final single, much like a contest.

Methods Not Recommended

Forced Repetitions with a Barbell—This method leads to a gain in muscle mass that may not be conducive to running or jumping improvement. This is due to adding unnecessary bodyweight in body parts that don't contribute to sport specific actions.

Maximal Eccentrics—This method calls for the athlete to lower a weight that could be 30 percent to 40 percent greater than their maximum barbell exercises, meaning squatting, pulling, or pressing movements. This is done with the help of spotters who will assist in returning the bar to the rack. If one likes, he or she may lower the barbell onto rack pins set at the bottom of the movement. Regardless, the barbell will gain speed as the body's leverage is at its weakest in the lowest positions. Example: if one performs a one-quarter squat, he or she could handle more than she would be able to in a half or full squat. The overloading in the bottom doing maximum eccentrics can be very dangerous, carrying a high risk of injury. If one chooses to do maximal eccentrics, you should attach strong rubber bands to the barbell. As one lowers the barbell, the bands lose some tension causing the load to be somewhat lighter, but will return to its original strength at the top position of the lift. When thinking about elasticity, refer to Hooke's Law.

Almost All Bodybuilding Programs—Bodybuilding programs include split routines and supersets. Repetitions to failure with light weights work for long runs, such as endurance races. Small special exercises can be used to near failure with good results, but never large barbell exercises.

Summing Up

Running fast or long distances requires one to master perfect form. Enlist weight training and lastly, jumping. This must be used throughout the yearly plan, adding what is needed and reducing what is not needed. Please reduce running and add more weight training. Using jumps to build explosive power, weights to increase absolute strength, and perfect form, you will become better at any distance. When using weight training, you must train at three velocities. If you choose to ignore one of these special strength velocities, you will fail. It is much like if you were to not use first gear when driving your car. You would start out slowly. If you did not use second gear, you would not accelerate. And if you did not have top gear, you could not maintain top speed. I hope this analogy helps you understand how important it is to use all special strengths, while maintaining top running form or working towards that goal.

The weight program may be done in 45 minutes, including jumping if short rest intervals, meaning 90 second rests, are utilized. This leaves the athlete lots of time to work on running form in its entirety. Most coaches will focus on top speed and acceleration, as this is roughly 60 percent of the 100-meter race. But, a better reaction time and block clearance can win a close race. Don't forget, many suffer from deceleration and lose the race at the finish line.

I trained a 60-meter Big Ten champ when his best time in the 100 meter was 10.47. His head coach said he would never run any faster. The athlete chose to train with me for nine weeks and ran a 10.17. How? We did it by applying the information within this book. He was terrible in his last 40 meters. He obviously lacked speed strength endurance. He improved it by powerwalking with a weight sled loaded to approximate bodyweight, 180 pounds, for 15 second powerwalks. Each week, he did 10 trips starting at 15 seconds per trip. The time was reduced until he covered 60 meters in an average time of 11 seconds. This was done on Wednesday. On Monday, he pulled a heavy sled loaded to 270 pounds for eight trips. This made it possible for him to be strong enough to pull his bodyweight at a continuous faster pace. Sixty jumps per workout were performed. Speed strength squatting and deadlifting were done before the powerwalking to act as a contrast method. For special exercises, reverse hypers, glute-ham raises, and leg raises were done for the posterior chain at the end of the workout. No bodyweight gain happened, but his absolute strength gained considerably.

While training world-record-holder Butch Reynolds for the 1996 Olympic trails in the 400 meter the training was similar in all aspects, according to the time of his race, which was roughly 43 seconds. The 400-meter requires all special strength and the ability to maintain top velocity. He would fade at the 300-meter to ensure that he had a finishing kick. I felt this was as much mental as physical. He pulled a weighted sled loaded to 225 pounds, close to his bodyweight, for 50 second walks. A runner was pitted next to him and would stay close until the 40-second period, then accelerate, as a way to force him to keep pace. This builds great speed endurance for the entire race and proved to Butch he could hold top speed throughout the last stages of the race. When using weight training for the 400 meter, the following was performed: belt squatting for 60 seconds with a rep per second, for five sets, with 2½ minute rest intervals. Mo Robinson, another 400-meter gold medalist, also used this protocol for maintaining maximum velocity. The belt squats were done with a very fast eccentrics phase, sitting onto a foam block, at about four-inches above parallel. A lot of glute, hamstring, and hip work was performed for special exercises. Much of their running work was reduced and special strength training was introduced in its place.

A third example is with a high school female who was brought to Westside. Her bodyweight was 117 pounds with an eight-second 60-meter, and a 34-inch box jump. After five months of training, her box jump went up to 48 inches for three sets of three jumps, and her 60-meter dropped to 7.24. She specialized in the 200 meter, with an initial 25 second time. After five months, she ran it in 23.85 and received a full-ride college scholarship. Now for the bad news, after entering college track, her times became slower and slower, and she incurred lower leg injuries as well as a hamstring pull. This should never happen. But, when a track coach has little knowledge as to what makes one run faster, it does happen. There is no excuse for this. A coach must learn all training aspects of running. Read, read, and read some more to gain knowledge and experience from the experts.

Watch a young boy, say 12-years-old, run for the first time all out. How did he run at all, if he had never ran before? The answer is due to other physical activity. Not running. There are many misconnections. One, building explosive power. The local football team will do power cleans to mistakenly build explosive power when the reality is that jumping in many forms builds the explosive power. The greatest experts on explosive power—such as Starzynski, Sozanski, Lasocki, and of course Verkhoshansky—do not discuss Olympic-style lifting for explosive power. They can only work in the 30 percent to 40 percent range for that is where the velocity for explosive strength is trained. Such velocity is fast velocity. If you look at the muscle recruitment pattern of the clean or snatch as an exercise, it is suited for Olympic weightlifters.

Westside writes books for the sole purpose of educating coaches in a subject matter they may have little knowledge in. The author was once talking about Verkhoshansky to a D1 strength coach who has won national championships in football and he did not know who Verkhoshansky was. At that point the conversation was ended, on the author's preference, as it was very clear how little he knew. Thank goodness for good recruiters. On the same note, Westside is at the top for developing all special strength, but we are not the experts on running, so we suggest to the reader to read the books listed in the references, over and over again.

Selected Bibliography & References

Allerheiligen. *Science of Sports Training*. (1994).
Biddle, Stuart J. H. *European Perspectives on Exercise and Sport Psychology*. (1995).
Bondarchuk, A. P. *Transfer of Training in Sports*.
  Michigan: Ultimate Athletic Concepts. (2007).
Bondarchuk, A. P. *Transfer of Training in Sports II*.
  Michigan: Ultimate Athletic Concepts, (2010).
Bondarchuk, A. P. *The Olympian Manual for Strength & Size*
  Michigan: Ultimate Athletic Concepts. (2014).
Bompa, T. *Power Training for Sports*. Champaign, Ill.: Human Kinetics. (1995).
Bompa, T. *Theory and Methodology of Training*. Champaign, Ill.: Human Kinetics. (1983).
Chu, Donald A. *Explosive Power & Strength* Champaign, Ill.: Human Kinetics, (1996).
Daniels, J. Human Kinetics. pp. 80-82. (1991).
Fraley, Bob & Jacoby, Ed *Complete Book of Jumps*. Champaign, Ill.: Human Kinetics, (1995).
Fizkultura *I Spovt, Physical Culture and Sports*. (1985).
Komi, P.V. *Strength and Power in Sport*. Great Britain, Blackwell Science Ltd, (1992).
Komi & Buskiak. Ergonomics. pp. 15, 417-434. (1972).
Kurz, T. Science of Sports Training. Island Pont, VT: Stadion, (1990).
Romanov, N., PhD. *The Pose Method of Running*. USA: Pose Tech Press, (2002).
Romanov, N., PhD. *Training Essays Volume 1*. USA: Pose Tech Press, (2006).
Ross, Barry. *Underground Secrets to Faster Running*. Lexington, Ky.: Bear Powered Publishing, (2005).
Rogers, Joseph L. *USA Track & Field Coaching Manual*. Champaign, Il. (2000)
Sherrington, C. *The Integrative Action of the Nervous System: A Centenary Appreciation*. (1906).
Schmolinsky, G. *Track and Field: The East German Textbook of Athletics*. Toronto, Ontario: Sports Book Publishers, (2006).
Schmolinsky, G. *Track and Field*. Berlin, Germany: Sportverlag, (1982).
Siff, Mel C. *Facts and Fallacies of Fitness*. Denver Co.: Supertraining Institute, (2000).
Siff, M. *Supertraining*. Denver, Co.: Supertraining Institute, (2003).
Siff, M. *Supertraining*. Denver, Co.: Supertraining Institute, (2004).
Silvester, Jay. *Complete Book of Throws*. Champaign, Ill: Human Kinetics, (2003).
Simmons, L. *Westside Barbell Book of Methods*. Ford du Lac, Wi: Action Printing, (2007).
Papanov, V. Sprinters from the G.D.A. Leg Kaya Atletika. Soviet Sports Review. 8:16-18. (1987).

S. H. Westing. European Journal of Applied Science. (1988).
Winter, Bud & Lee, Jimson *The Rocket Sprint Start*. USA: Bud Winter Enterprises, (2011).
Winter, Bud *SO YOU WANT TO BE A SPRINTER*.
USA: Bud Winter Enterprises, (2010).
Winter, Bud *RELAX and WIN*. USA: Bud Winter Enterprises, (2012).
Yessis, M. *Biomechanics and Kinesiology of Exercise*.
Michigan: Ultimate Athletic Concepts, (2013).
Yessis, M. *Secrets of Soviet Sports Fitness and Training*.
Michigan: Ultimate Athletic Concepts, (1987).
Yessis, M. *Soviet Sports Review. Volume 19, Number 2*
Michigan: Ultimate Athletic Concepts, (1984).
Yessis, M. *Soviet Sports Review. Volume 19, Number 3*
Michigan: Ultimate Athletic Concepts, (1984).
Yessis, M. *Soviet Sports Review. Volume 20, Number 1*
Michigan: Ultimate Athletic Concepts, (1985).
Yessis, M. *Soviet Sports Review. Volume 20, Number 2*
Michigan: Ultimate Athletic Concepts, (1985).
Yessis, M. *Soviet Sports Review. Volume 20, Number 3*
Michigan: Ultimate Athletic Concepts, (1985).
Yessis, M. *Soviet Sports Review. Volume 20, Number 4*
Michigan: Ultimate Athletic Concepts, (1985).
Yessis, M. *Soviet Sports Review. Volume 21, Number 3*
Michigan: Ultimate Athletic Concepts, (1986).
Yessis, M. *Soviet Sports Review. Volume 21, Number 4*
Michigan: Ultimate Athletic Concepts, (1986).
Yessis, M. *Soviet Sports Review. Volume 22, Number 1*
Michigan: Ultimate Athletic Concepts, (1987).
Yessis, M. *Soviet Sports Review. Volume 22, Number 2*
Michigan: Ultimate Athletic Concepts, (1987).
Yessis, M. *Soviet Sports Review. Volume 22, Number 4*
Michigan: Ultimate Athletic Concepts, (1988).
Yessis, M. *Soviet Sports Review. Volume 24, Number 1*
Michigan: Ultimate Athletic Concepts, (1989).
Zatsiorsky, V.M. *Science and Practice of Strength Training*.
Champaign, IL: Human Kinetics, (1995).

www.ingramcontent.com/pod-product-compliance
Lightning Source LLC
Chambersburg PA
CBHW050109170426
43198CB00014B/2508